Best Editorial Cartoons of the Year

Q. WHAT DO YOU CALL IT WHEN YOU KILL INNOCENT MEN, WOMEN AND CHILDREN?

A.

A HOLY WAR.

BEST EDITORIAL CARTOONS OF THE YEAR

2002 EDITION

Edited by
CHARLES BROOKS

PELICAN PUBLISHING COMPANY
Gretna 2002

Library of Congress Serial Catalog Data

Best Editorial Cartoons, 1972-
  Gretna [La.] Pelican Pub. Co.
  v. 30 cm annual-
"A pictorial history of the year."

  1. United States—Politics and government—
1969—Caricatures and Cartoons—Periodicals.
E839.5.B45 320.9'7309240207   73-643645
ISSN 0091-2220   MARC-S

Manufactured in the United States of America
Published by Pelican Publishing Company, Inc.
1000 Burmaster Street, Gretna, Louisiana 70053

Contents

Award-Winning Cartoons

2001 PULITZER PRIZE

8/29/00   ©2000 Dist. by Los Angeles Times Syndicate   ATelnaes@AOL.COM

ANN TELNAES

Editorial Cartoonist
Tribune Media Services

Born in Stockholm, Sweden; graduate of the California Institute of the Arts, with a specialty in character animation; former artist for Walt Disney Imagineering and various animation studios in London, Los Angeles, Taiwan, and New York; the second woman to win the Pulitzer Prize for editorial cartooning.

2000 NATIONAL SOCIETY OF
PROFESSIONAL JOURNALISTS AWARD
(Selected in 2001)

NICK ANDERSON

Editorial Cartoonist
Louisville Courier-Journal

Born in Toledo, Ohio, 1967; majored in political science and was editorial cartoonist for the university newspaper at Ohio State University; winner of the Charles M. Schulz Award for the best college cartoonist, 1989; associate editorial cartoonist *Louisville Courier-Journal,* 1991, and chief editorial cartoonist, 1995 to the present; winner of the John Fischetti Award for editorial cartoons, 1999. The names of his sons, Colton and Travis, are hidden in all of his cartoons.

STEVE KELLEY

Editorial Cartoonist
San Diego Union-Tribune

Born in Richmond, Virginia; graduated from Dartmouth College, 1981; editorial cartoonist for the *San Diego Union-Tribune,* 1981 to 2001; maintains an active speaking schedule as a humorist.

2000 SCRIPPS-HOWARD FOUNDATION NATIONAL JOURNALISM AWARD

(Selected in 2001)

JAMES CASCIARI

Editorial Cartoonist
Vero Beach Press Journal

Born in Wilton, Connecticut; graduated from the University of Miami; editorial cartoonist for the *Vero Beach Press Journal,* 1991 to the present, and the Treasure Coast Newspapers (*The Stuart News, The Port St. Lucie News,* and *The Fort Pierce Tribune),* 1996 to the present; winner of the Florida Press Club Excellence in Journalism Award for editorial cartooning, 1998, 1999, 2000, and 2001.

2001 BERRYMAN AWARD

JOE LIEBERMAN COMES TO SOUTH FLORIDA.

CHAN LOWE

Editorial Cartoonist
Fort Lauderdale Sun-Sentinel

Born in New York City, 1953; graduated from Williams College, 1975; editorial cartoonist for the *Shawnee* (Oklahoma) *News-Star,* 1975-77, the *Oklahoma City Times,* 1978-84, and the *Fort Lauderdale Sun-Sentinel,* 1984 to the present; an occasional feature writer, television columnist, and classical music critic; cartoons syndicated by Tribune Media Services.

(The Pope embraces Palestinian soil. Yasser Arafat presents him a plate of the soil, saying: "That's all of it we can find at the moment.")

SERGE CHAPLEAU

Editorial Cartoonist
La Presse (Montreal)

Born in Montreal, 1945; newspaper caricaturist for various publications since 1971; previous winner of Canada's National Newspaper Award for editorial cartooning in 1997 and 1999.

Best Editorial Cartoons of the Year

J.D. CROWE
Courtesy Mobile Register

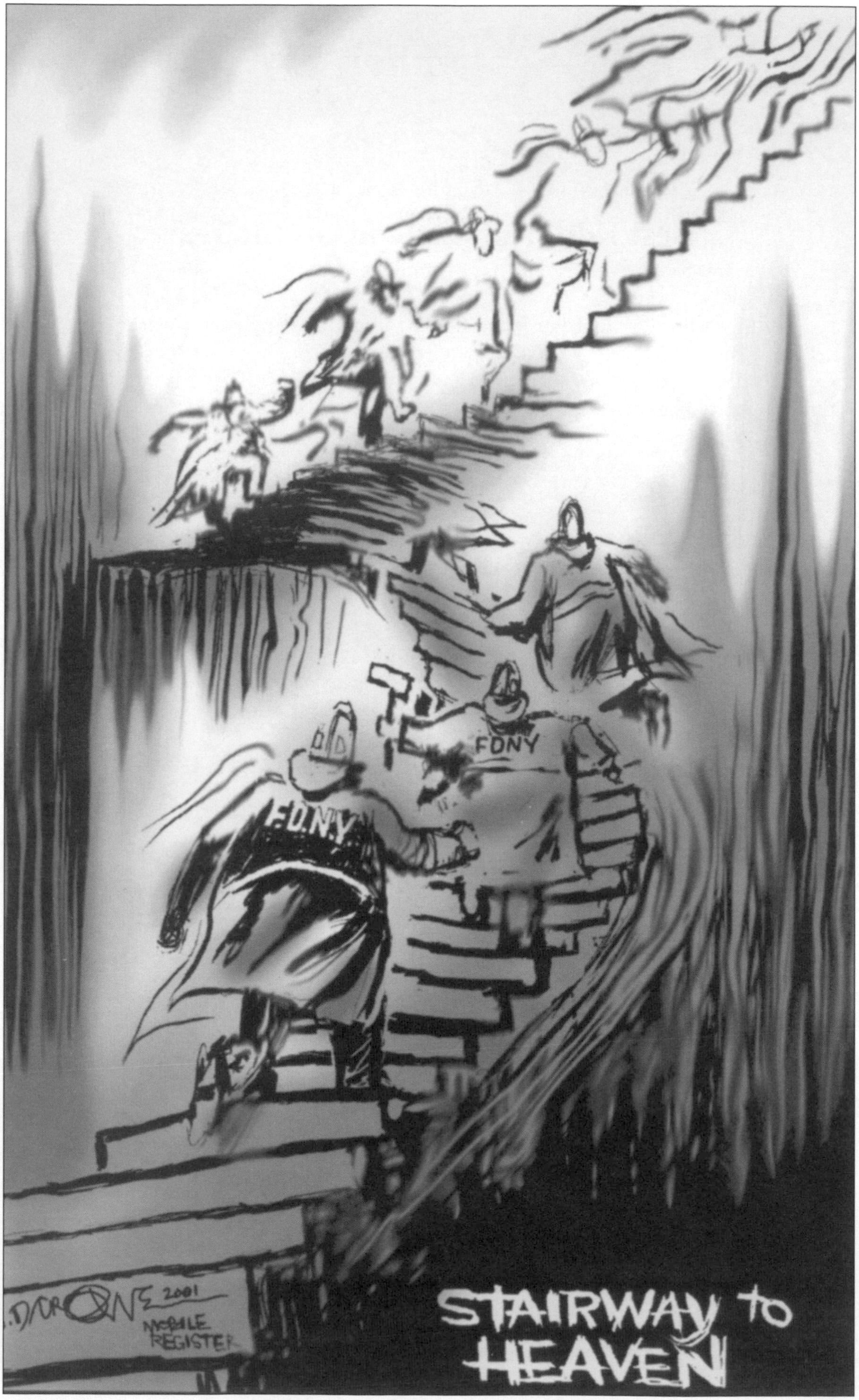
F.D.N.Y
FDNY
J.D. CROWE 2001
MOBILE REGISTER
STAIRWAY to HEAVEN

September 11

On September 11, another day that will live in infamy, several thousand people were killed in a devastating terrorist attack in New York City and Washington, D.C. Two hijacked passenger planes were deliberately crashed into the World Trade Center Towers in New York, and the 1,350-foot buildings collapsed within an hour because of the extreme heat from burning jet fuel.

A third hijacked airplane slammed into the Pentagon in Washington, while a fourth, possibly headed for the White House or the Capitol, crashed in the Pennsylvania countryside when passengers resisted their hijackers.

Suspicion immediately fell on Islamic terrorist Osama bin Laden, whose organization had been responsible for bombings in Africa and the attack on the *USS Cole.* President George W. Bush labeled the attack an act of war and vowed to confront terrorism wherever it could be found.

Among the first real American heroes of the new century were the courageous New York City firemen and police officers who plunged into the inferno trying to assist victims. An estimated 400 firefighters and some 40 police officers were entombed when the skyscrapers collapsed.

CHUCK ASAY
Courtesy Colorado Springs Gazette-Telegraph

DAYS OF INFAMY !

Dec. 7, 1941   Sept. 11, 2001

JAMES CASCIARI
Courtesy Vero Beach Press Journal

JOHN SPENCER
Courtesy Philadelphia Business Journal

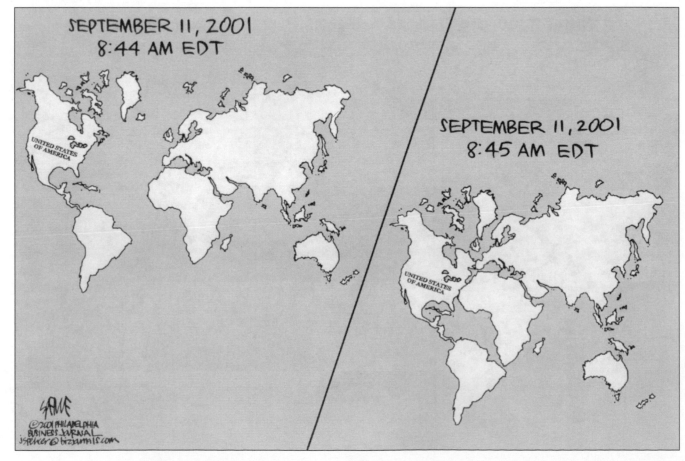

MARTY RISKIN
Courtesy Georgetown Record (Mass.)

BRIAN DUFFY
Courtesy Des Moines Register

BOB GORRELL
Courtesy Creators Syndicate

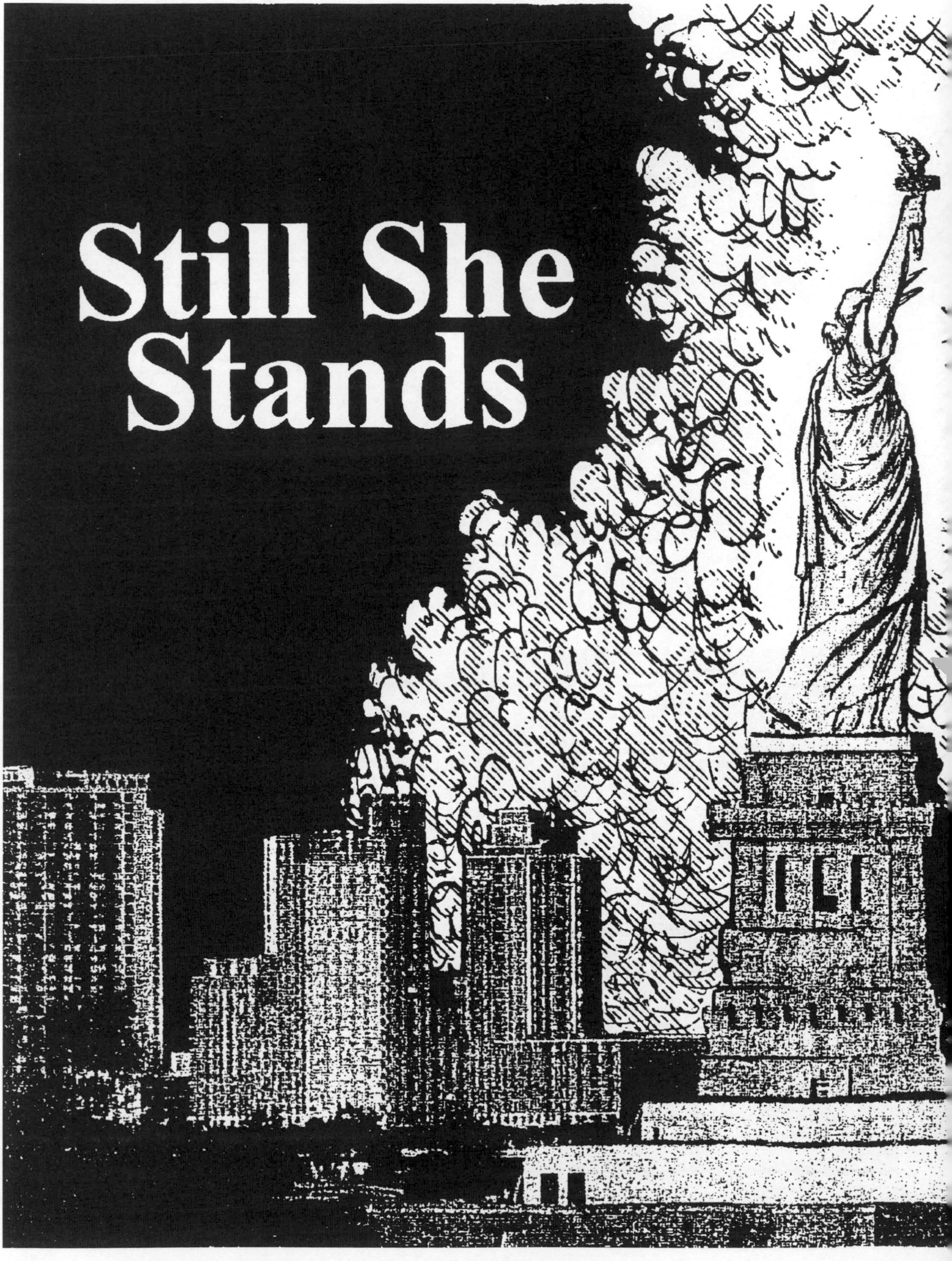
Still She
Stands

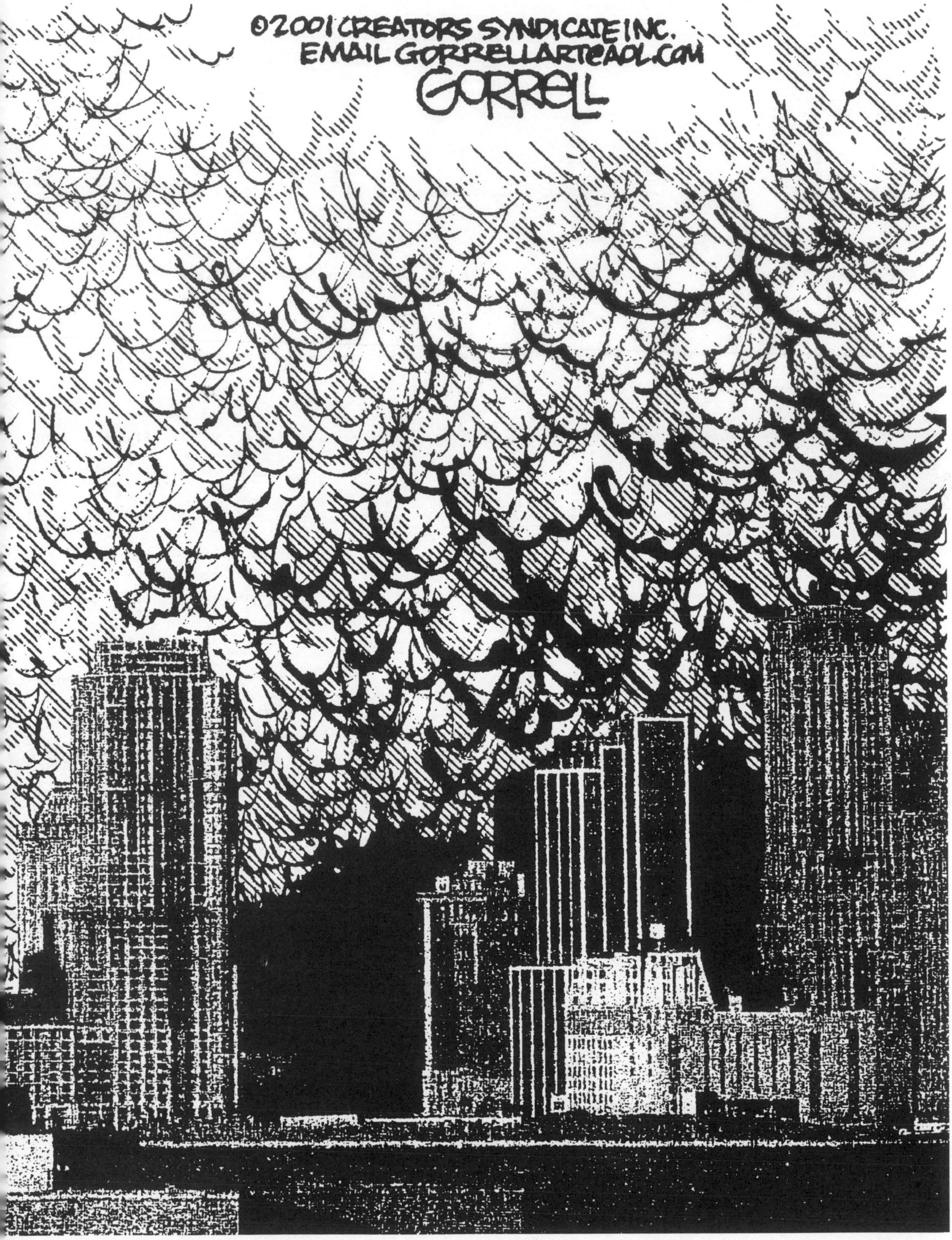
©2001 CREATORS SYNDICATE INC.
EMAIL GORRELLART@AOL.COM
GORRELL

S.C. RAWLS
Courtesy Rockdale Citizen

JOHN SHERFFIUS
Courtesy St. Louis Post-Dispatch

STUART CARLSON
Courtesy Milwaukee Journal-Sentinel

TIM BENSON
Courtesy Argus-Leader (S.D.)

21

JIM BERRY
Courtesy NEA

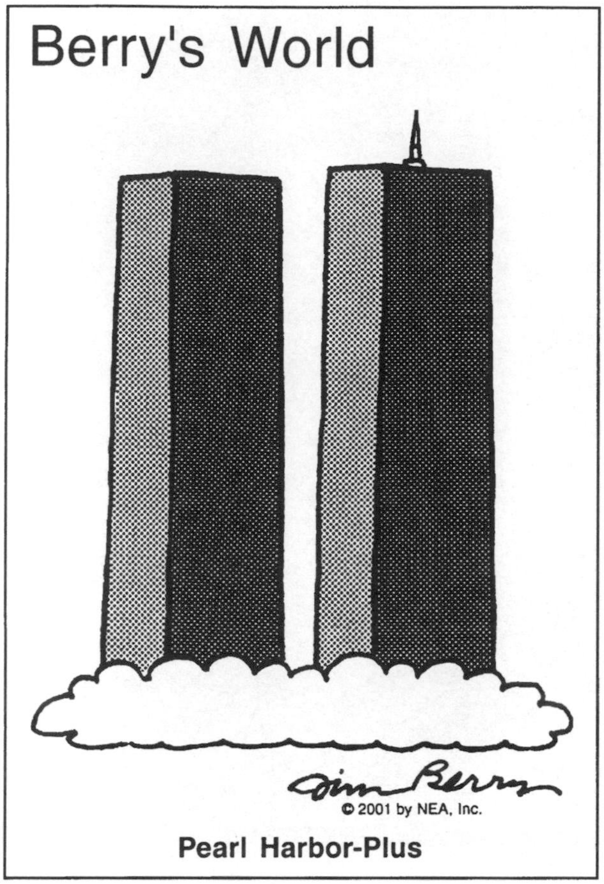

Berry's World
Jim Berry
© 2001 by NEA, Inc.
Pearl Harbor-Plus

STEVE NEASE
Courtesy London Free Press (Can.)

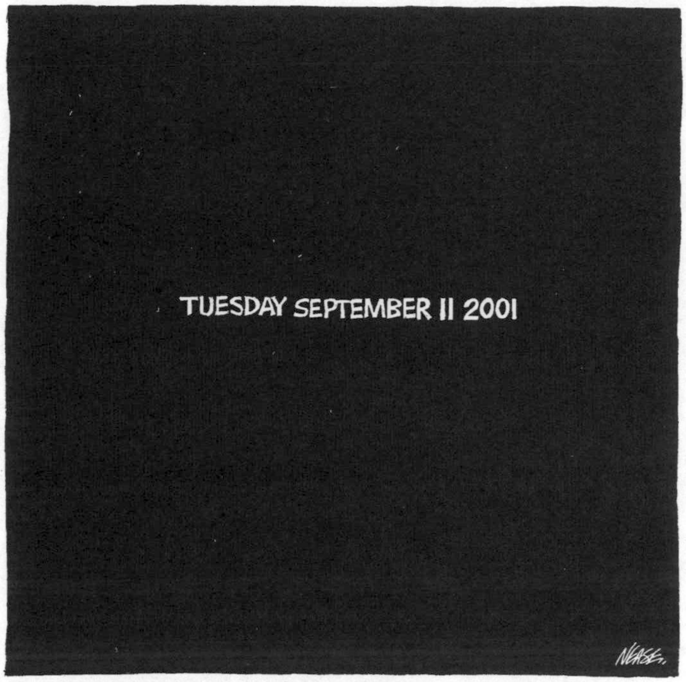

TUESDAY SEPTEMBER 11 2001
NEASE

TOMMY THOMPSON
Courtesy San Diego Union-Tribune

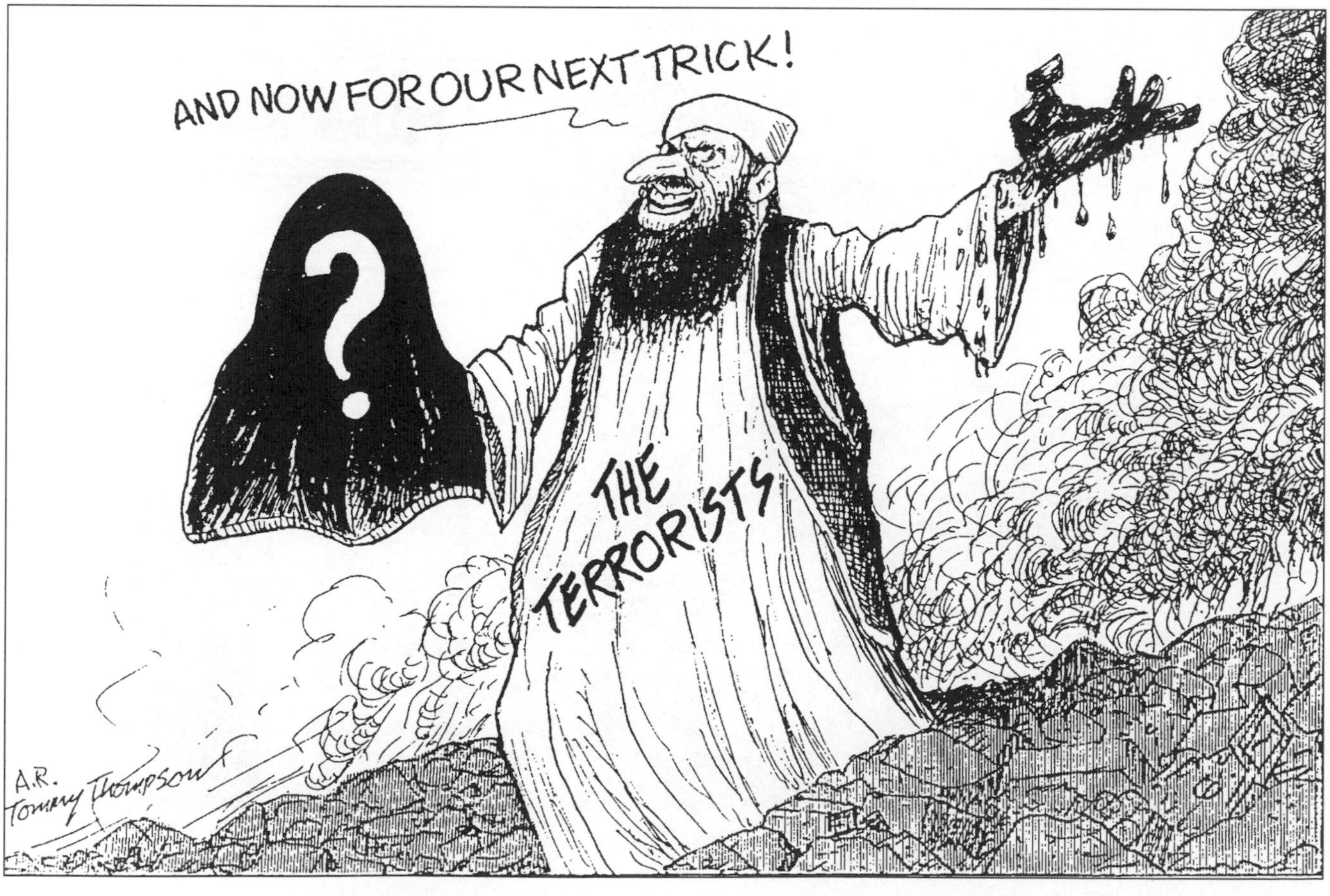

AND NOW FOR OUR NEXT TRICK!
THE TERRORISTS
A.R. Tommy Thompson

JAMES McCLOSKEY
Courtesy Daily News Leader (Va.)

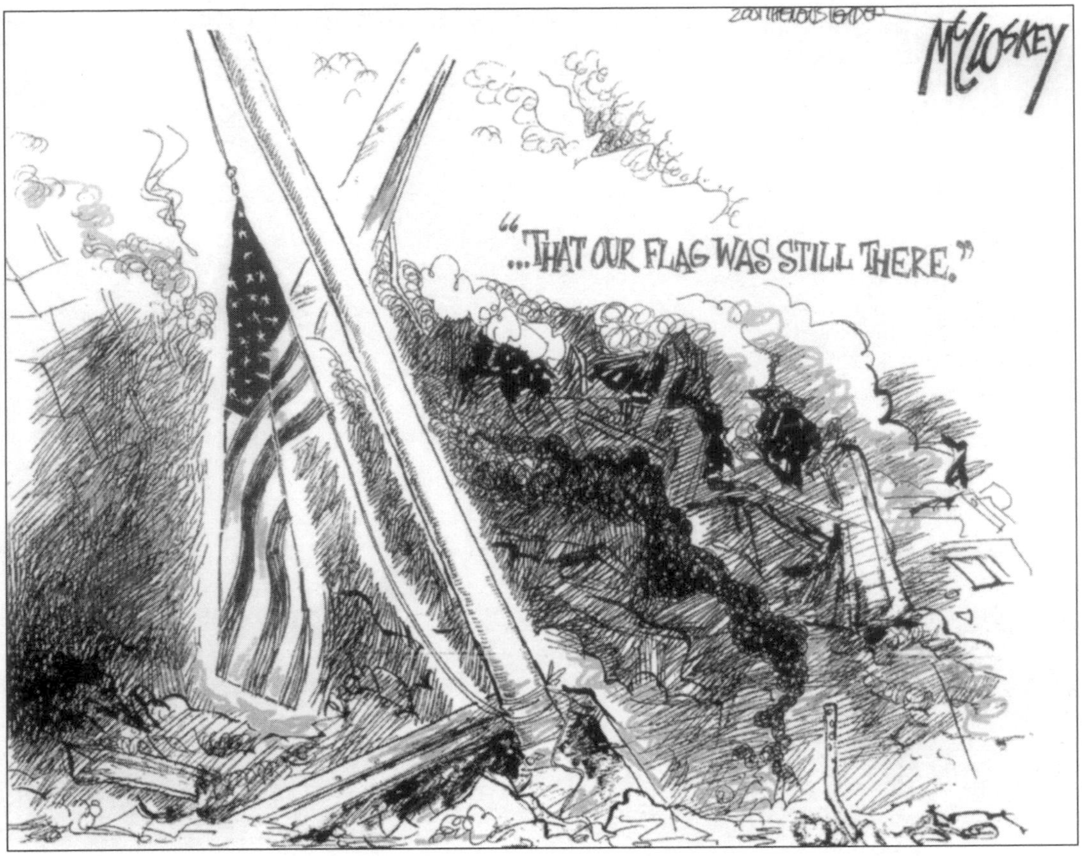
McCLOSKEY
"...THAT OUR FLAG WAS STILL THERE."

STEVE KELLEY
Courtesy San Diego Union-Tribune

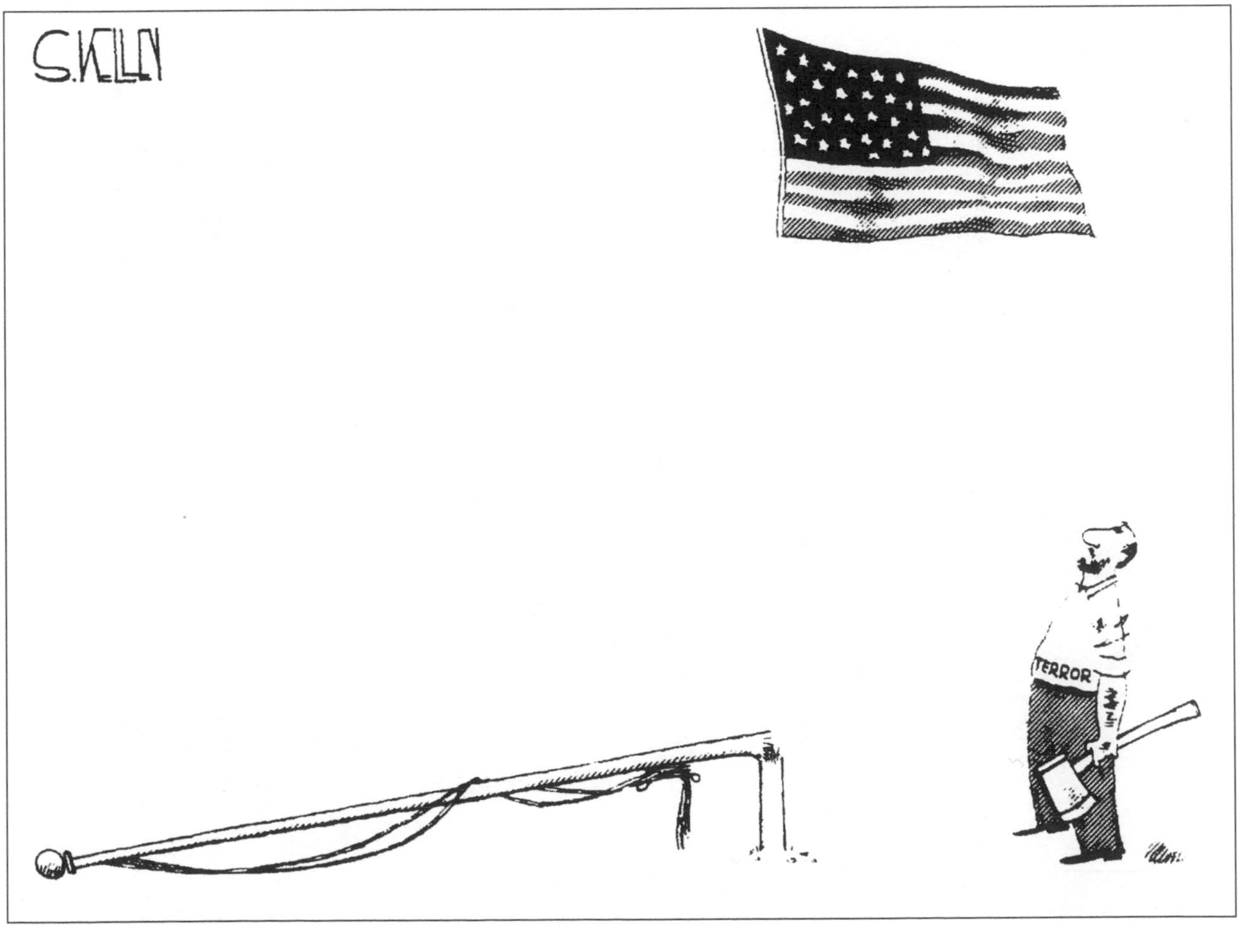
S.KELLEY
TERROR

JACK HIGGINS
Courtesy Chicago Sun-Times

MIKE LUCKOVICH
Courtesy Atlanta Constitution

CHESTER COMMODORE
Courtesy Chicago Defender

DREW SHENEMAN
Courtesy Newark Star-Ledger

RANDY BISH
Courtesy Tribune-Review (Pa.)

...ONE NATION UNDER GOD, INDIVISIBLE...

THE UNITED STATES OF AMERICA

LINDA BOILEAU
Courtesy Frankfort State Journal (Ky.)

FRED CURATOLO
Courtesy Edmonton Sun (Can.)

STEPHEN TEMPLETON
Courtesy Fayetteville Observer-Times

"so much owed by so many to so few"
- W. Churchill

DOUG MacGREGOR
Courtesy Fort Myers News-Press

JOHN SLADE
Courtesy Louisiana Weekly

JIM BERTRAM
Courtesy St. Cloud Times (Minn.)

WAYNE STAYSKAL
Courtesy Tampa Tribune

SERGE CHAPLEAU
Courtesy La Presse (Can.)

PAUL FELL
Courtesy Lincoln Journal Star (Neb.)

RICK McKEE
Courtesy Augusta Chronicle (Ga.)

VIC CANTONE
Courtesy Brooklyn Paper Publications

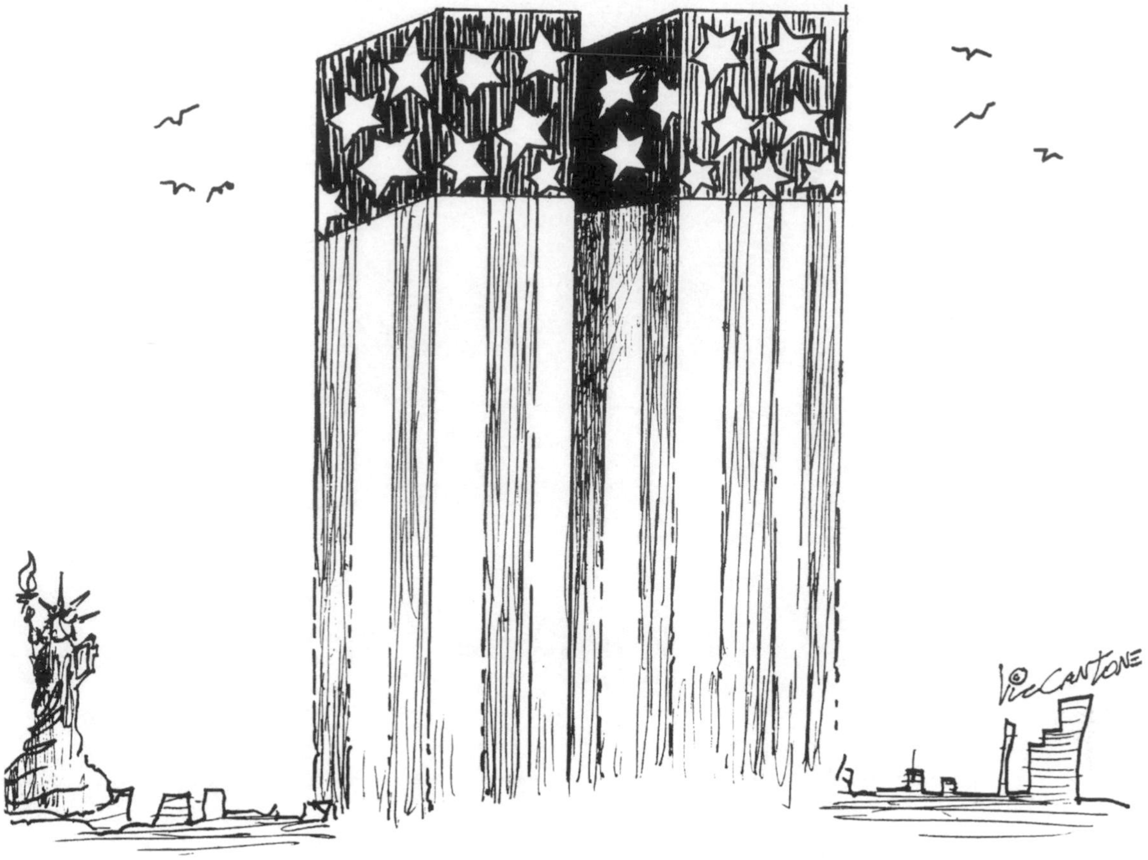

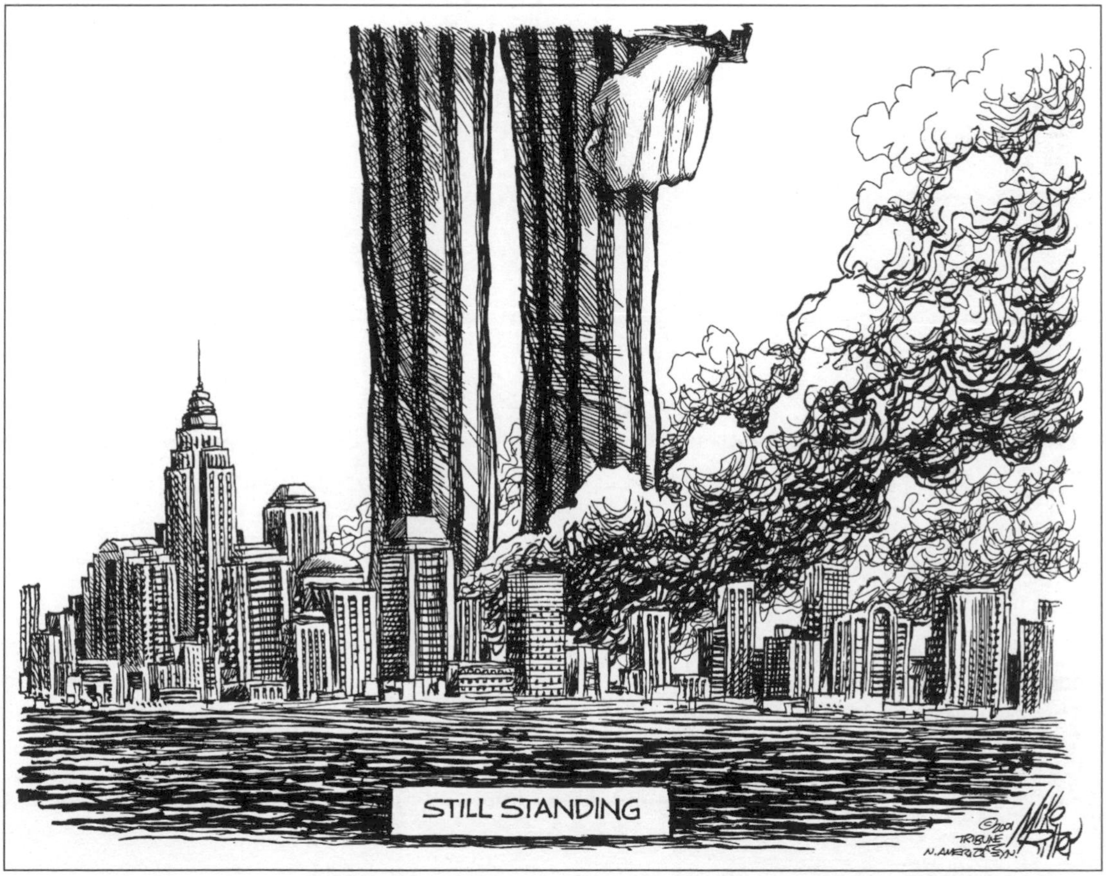
STILL STANDING

MIKE RITTER
Courtesy Tribune Newspapers

J.D. CROWE
Courtesy Mobile Register

DANI AGUILA
Courtesy Filipino Reporter

PAM WINTERS
Courtesy Stockton Record

Canyon of HEROES

JIMMY MARGULIES
Courtesy The Record (N.J.)

NICK ANDERSON
Courtesy Louisville Courier-Journal

DARYL CAGLE
Courtesy Slate.com

THE ROOT OF ALL EVIL

JIM LANGE
Courtesy The Daily Oklahoman

PETER DUNLAP-SHOHL
Courtesy Anchorage Daily News

MICHAEL OSBUN
Courtesy Citrus City Chronicle (Fla.)

DOUG REGALIA
Courtesy Contra Costa Sun

DANA SUMMERS
Courtesy Orlando Sentinel

GARY BROOKINS
Courtesy Richmond Times-Dispatch

THE ENEMY, 1941:

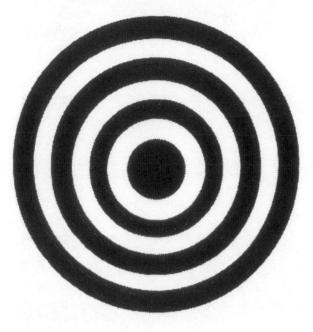

THE ENEMY, 2001:

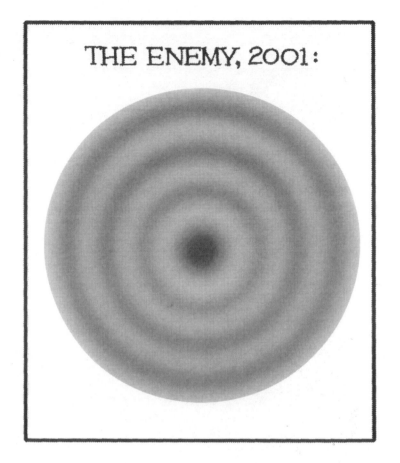

San Diego Union-Tribune ©2001
COPLEY NEWS SERVICE

STEVE BREEN
Courtesy San Diego Union-Tribune

MIKE PETERS ©2001 DAYTON DAILY NEWS TRIBUNE MEDIA SERVICES
grimmy.com

MIKE PETERS
Courtesy Dayton Daily News

FRED CURATOLO
Courtesy Edmonton Sun (Can.)

...Cry *Havoc*, and let slip the dogs of war;
That this foul deed shall smell above the earth
With carrion men, groaning for burial.
—SHAKESPEARE

BRUMSIC BRANDON, JR.
Courtesy Florida Today

STEVE LINDSTROM
Courtesy Duluth News-Tribune

CHARLES DANIEL
Courtesy Knoxville News-Sentinel

LAZARO FRESQUET
Courtesy El Nuevo Herald (Fla.)

STEVE McBRIDE
Courtesy Independence Daily Reporter (Kan.)

BILL GARNER
Courtesy Washington Times

RANAN LURIE
Courtesy Cartoonews International

Lurie's NewsCartoon

"I really think we should make an exception..."

MIKE PETERS
Courtesy Dayton Daily News

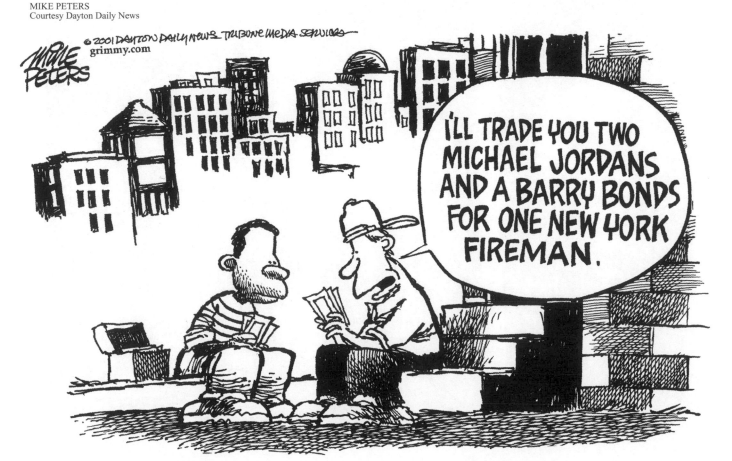

DON LANDGREN, JR.
Courtesy The Landmark (Mass.)

JERRY BARNETT
Courtesy Indianapolis Star

BILL GARNER
Courtesy Washington Times

GUY BADEAUX
Courtesy Le Droit (Can.)

DARYL CAGLE
Courtesy Slate.com

RANDY BISH
Courtesy Tribune-Review (Pa.)

THE BIGGEST HEROES DIDN'T HIT OVER 70 HOME RUNS THIS YEAR
(AND THEY DIDN'T ASK TO BE PAID MORE THAN $10 MILLION)

JACK JURDEN
Courtesy Wilmington News Journal

JACK HIGGINS
Courtesy Chicago Sun-Times

ED STEIN
Courtesy Rocky Mountain News

45

JEFF STAHLER
Courtesy Cincinnati Post

BRIAN DUFFY
Courtesy Des Moines Register

STEVE LINDSTROM
Courtesy Duluth News-Tribune

ROBERT ARIAIL
Courtesy The State (S.C.)

MIKE KEEFE
Courtesy Denver Post

The Response

Gaining the presidency by only a razor-thin margin and being portrayed by the media as none too bright, George W. Bush gained America's respect, support, and admiration for the way he responded to the September 11 terrorist attacks.

In the days immediately following the attacks, his approval rating quickly soared to 90 percent in polls, with even most Democrats acknowledging that he was doing a fine job. He fashioned a strong, almost unheard-of coalition that included a Labor prime minister of Great Britain, a Russian president, and a Pakistani dictator. Furthermore, he succeeded in uniting many countries around the globe in the fight against terrorism.

New York mayor Rudy Giuliani, too, performed magnificently in the wake of the unprecedented attack, rallying the city's citizens, leading the recovery effort, and strengthening their resolve.

As the year came to a close, Osama bin Laden, leader of the al Queda terror network, and his Taliban cronies were out of power and on the run in Afghanistan. Weeks of relentless airstrikes had taken a severe toll, and the opposition Northern Alliance had tightened its grip on what had been Taliban territory. At the same time, the U.S. began air-dropping hundreds of tons of food and supplies to the desperate Afghan citizenry.

WAYNE STROOT
Courtesy Hastings Tribune (Neb.)

49

ED GAMBLE
Courtesy Florida Times-Union

RANAN LURIE
Courtesy Cartoonews International

PAUL CONRAD
Courtesy Los Angeles Times Syndicate

JACK HIGGINS
Courtesy Chicago Sun-Times

BOB ENGLEHART
Courtesy Hartford Courant

JERRY HOLBERT
Courtesy Boston Herald

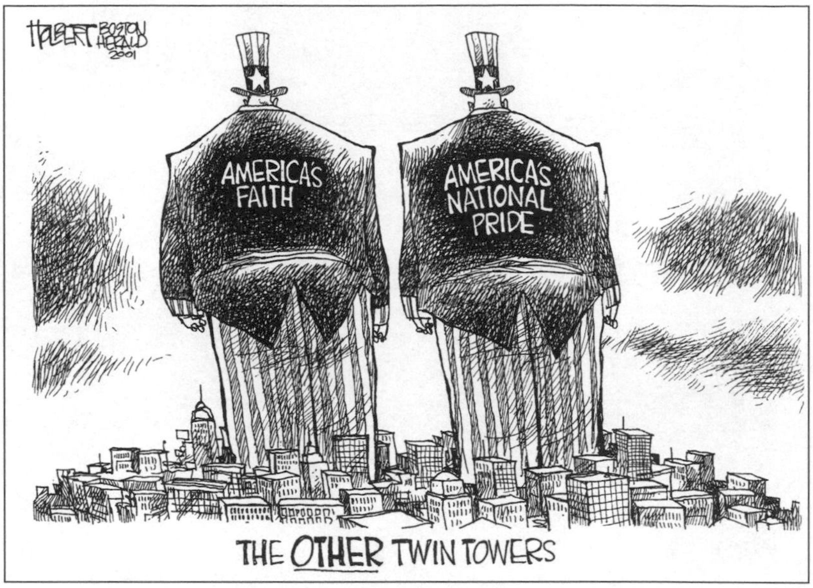
HOLBERT BOSTON HERALD 2001
AMERICA'S FAITH
AMERICA'S NATIONAL PRIDE
THE OTHER TWIN TOWERS

MICHAEL CAVNA
Courtesy San Diego Union-Tribune

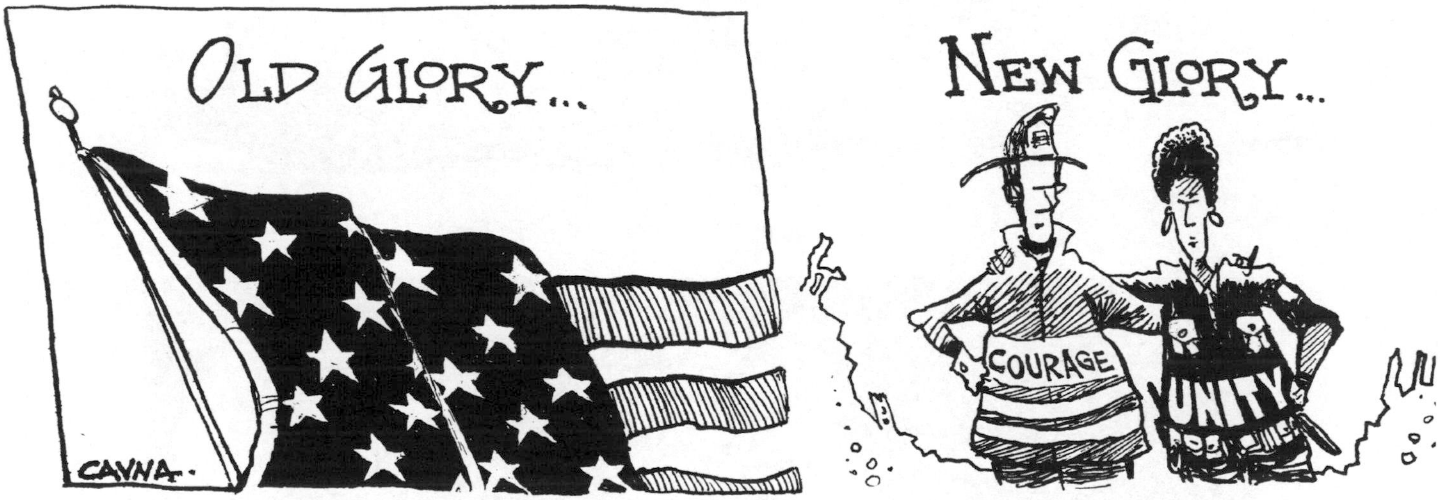
OLD GLORY...
CAVNA
NEW GLORY...
COURAGE
UNITY

JEFF KOTERBA
Courtesy Omaha World-Herald

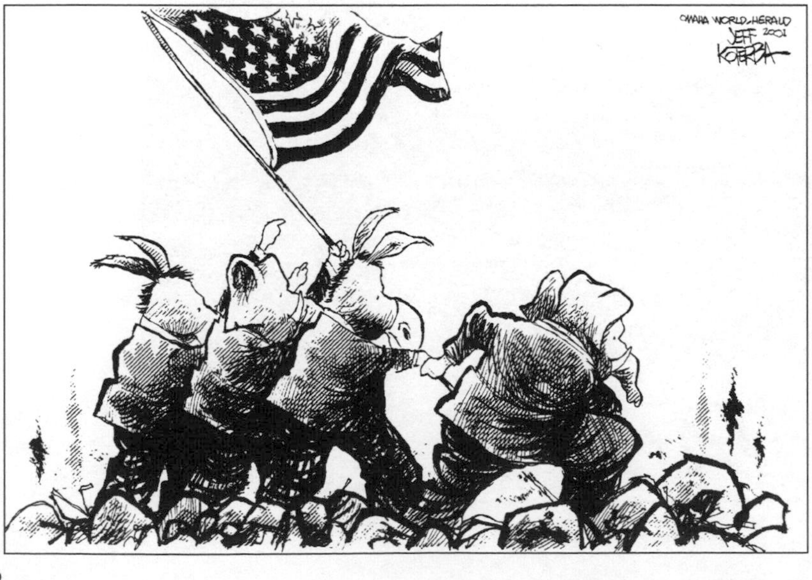
OMAHA WORLD-HERALD
JEFF 2001
KOTERBA

RICHARD CROWSON
Courtesy Wichita Eagle

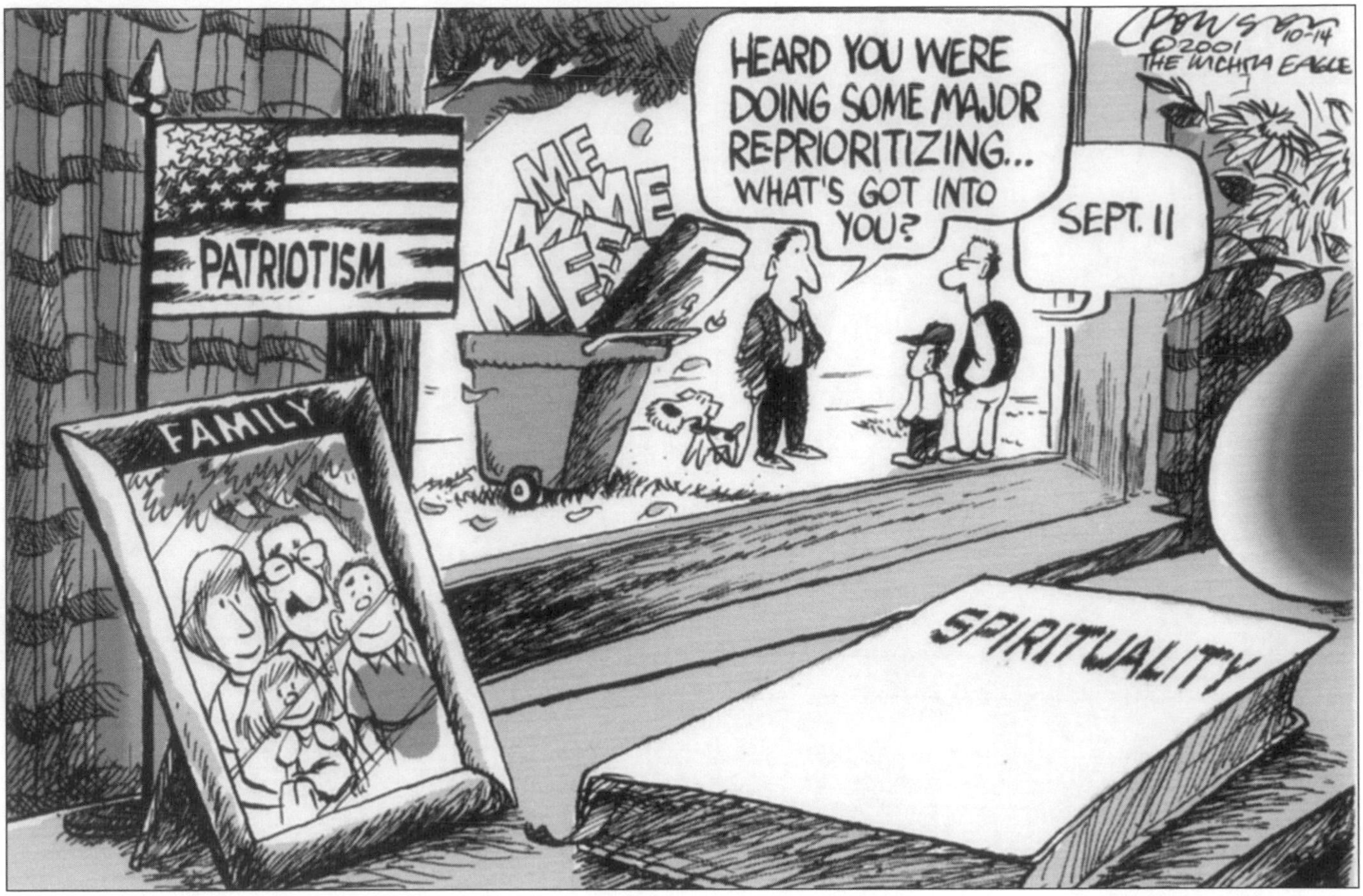

CROWSON 10-14 ©2001 THE WICHITA EAGLE
PATRIOTISM
ME ME ME ME
HEARD YOU WERE DOING SOME MAJOR RE-PRIORITIZING... WHAT'S GOT INTO YOU?
SEPT. 11
FAMILY
SPIRITUALITY

ROB HARRIMAN
Courtesy Portland Tribune

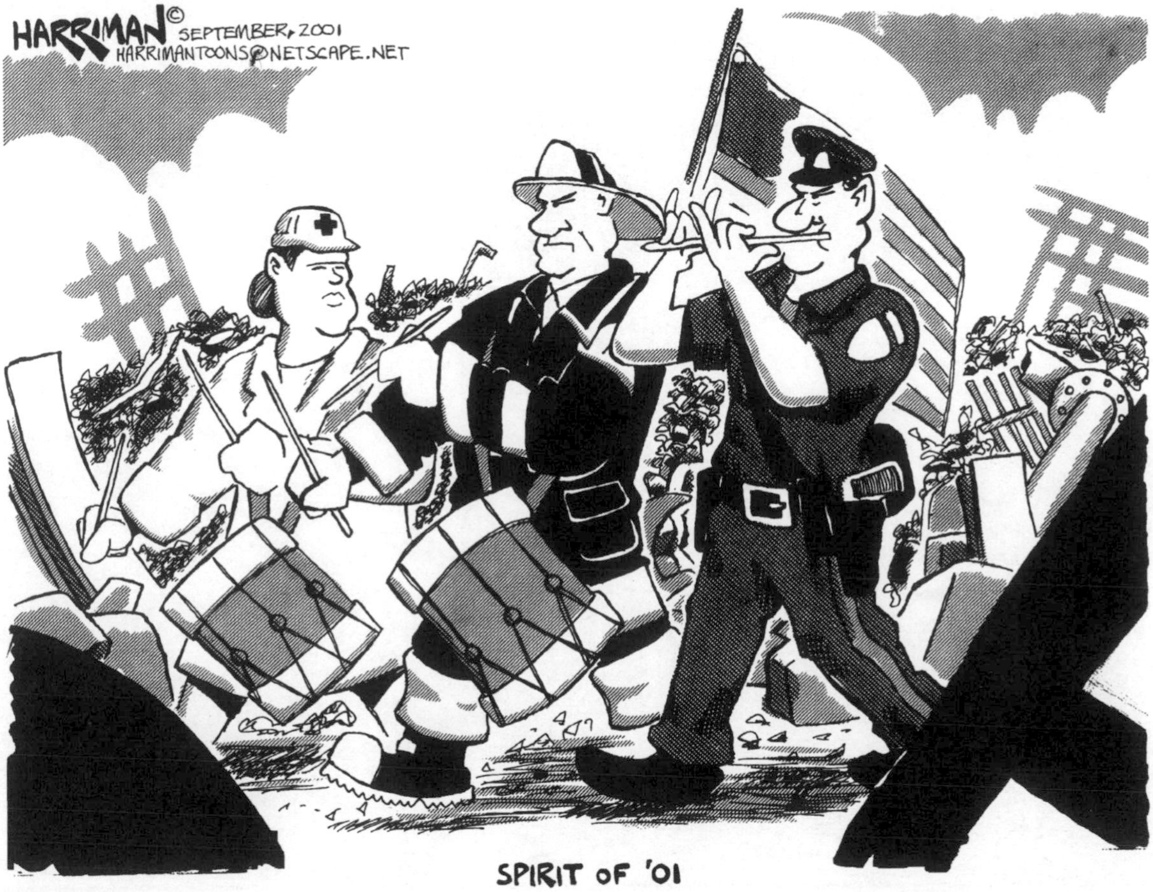

HARRIMAN© SEPTEMBER, 2001
HARRIMANTOONS@NETSCAPE.NET
SPIRIT OF '01

JACK JURDEN
Courtesy Wilmington News Journal

ANDY DONATO
Courtesy Toronto Sun

CLAY BENNETT
Courtesy Christian Science Monitor

54

JIM DYKE
Courtesy Jefferson City News-Tribune

DICK LOCHER
Courtesy Chicago Tribune

BILL GARNER
Courtesy Washington Times

ROY PETERSON
Courtesy Vancouver Sun

KEVIN KALLAUGHER
Courtesy Baltimore Sun

DOUG MacGREGOR
Courtesy Fort Myers News-Press

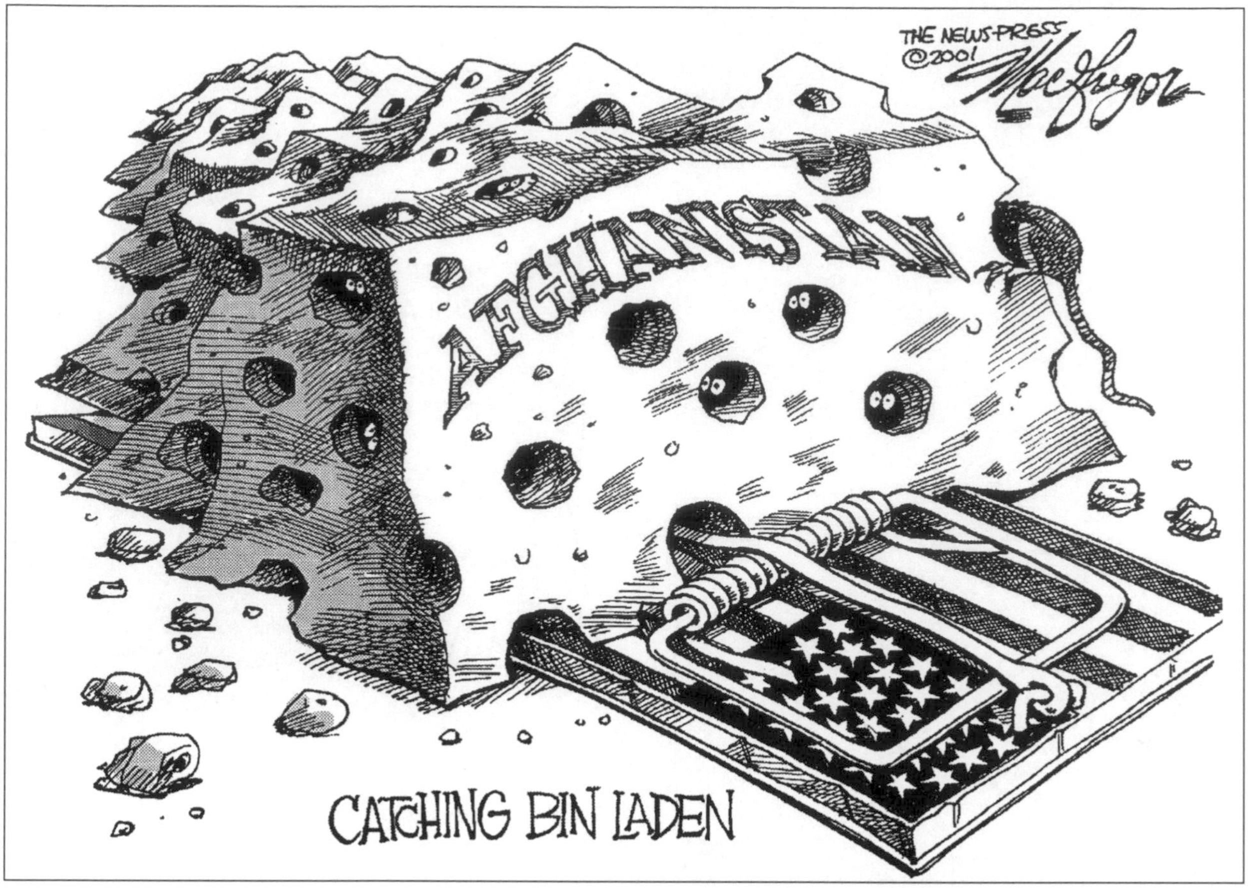
THE NEWS-PRESS ©2001
MacGregor
AFGHANISTAN
CATCHING BIN LADEN

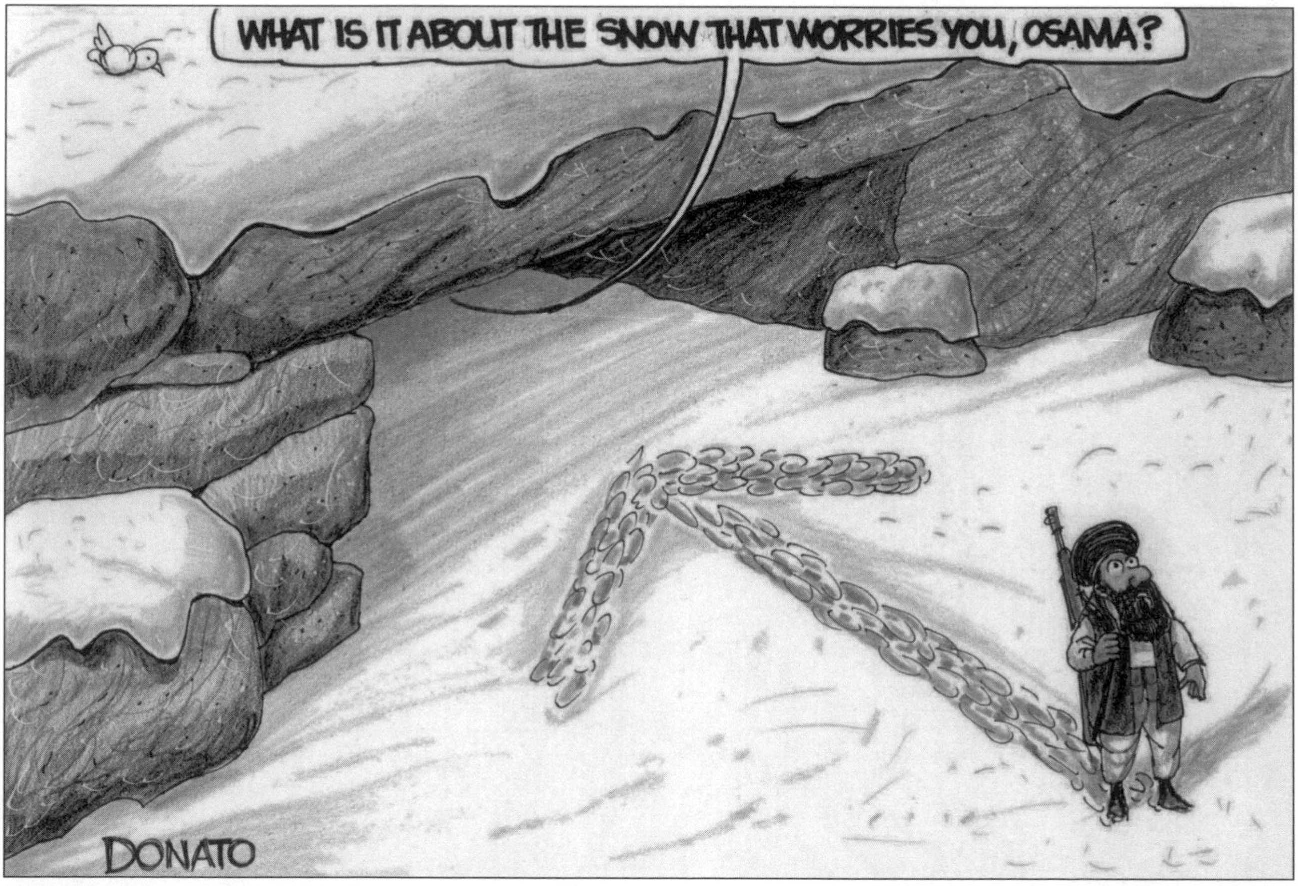
WHAT IS IT ABOUT THE SNOW THAT WORRIES YOU, OSAMA?
DONATO

ANDY DONATO
Courtesy Toronto Sun

RANAN LURIE
Courtesy Cartoonews International

LAZARO FRESQUET
Courtesy El Nuevo Herald (Fla.)

WALT HANDELSMAN
Courtesy Newsday

STANDING UP TO TERRORISM —

PAM WINTERS
Courtesy San Diego Union-Tribune

JERRY HOLBERT
Courtesy Boston Herald

JIM BORGMAN
Courtesy Cincinnati Enquirer

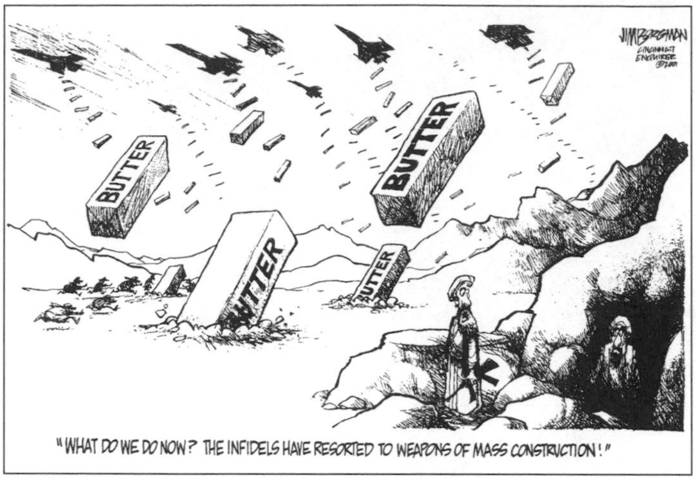
BUTTER
BUTTER
BUTTER
BUTTER
"WHAT DO WE DO NOW? THE INFIDELS HAVE RESORTED TO WEAPONS OF MASS CONSTRUCTION!"

GEORGE DANBY
Courtesy Bangor Daily News

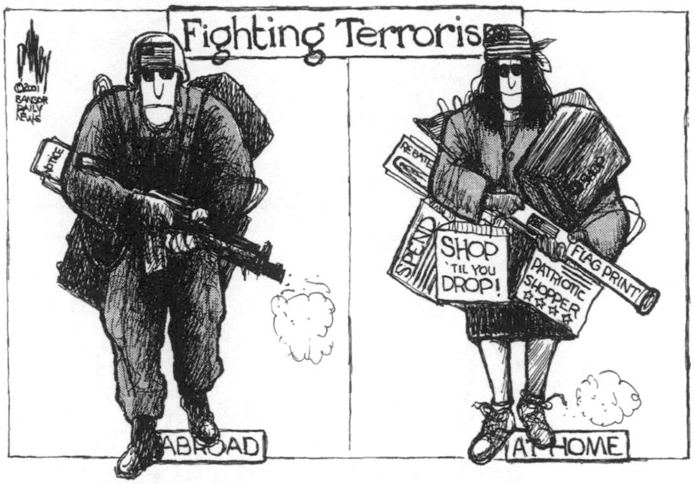
Fighting Terroris
ABROAD
AT HOME
REBATE
SPEND
SHOP 'TIL YOU DROP!
PATRIOTIC SHOPPER
FLAG PRINT

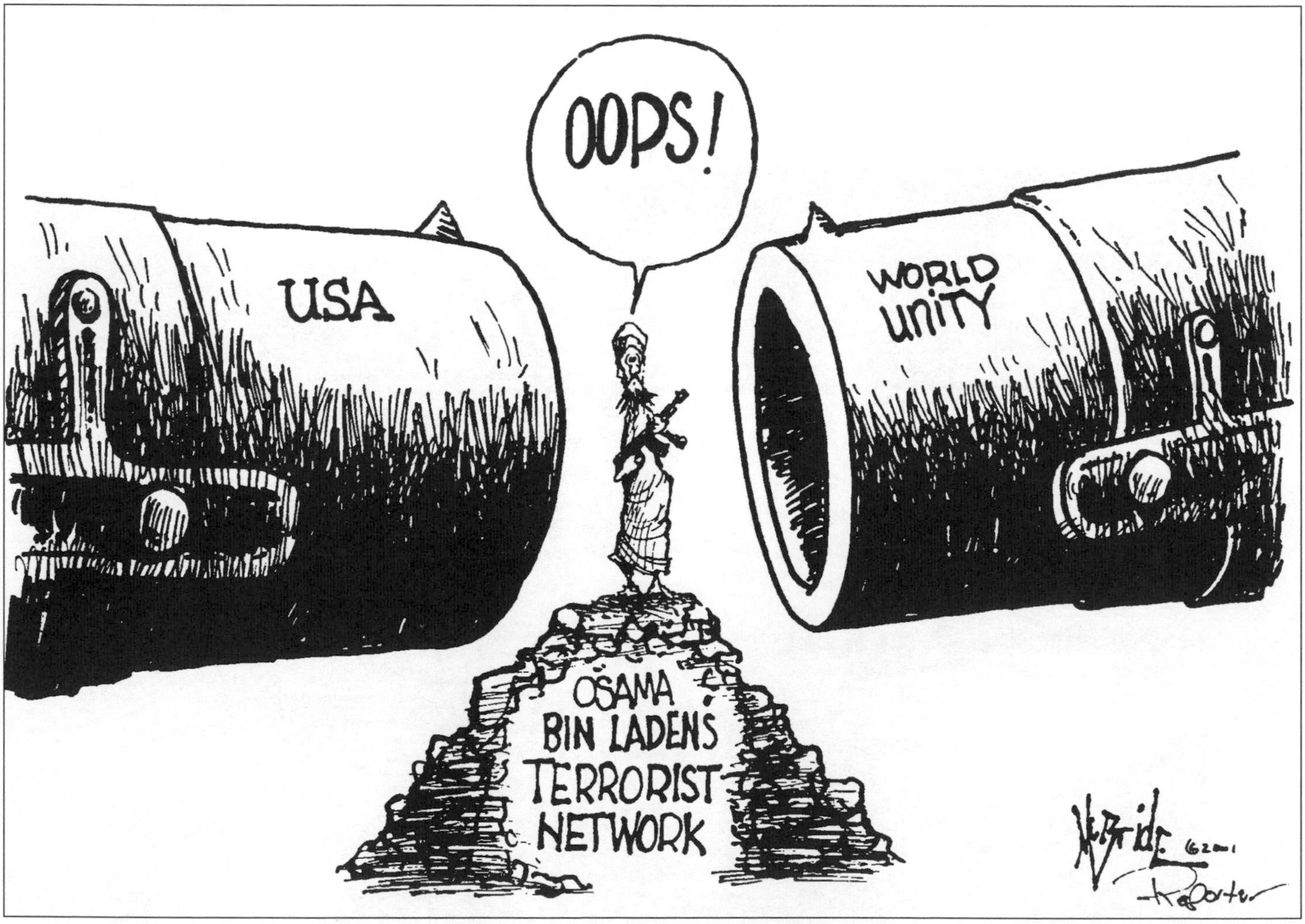
OOPS!
USA
WORLD UNITY
OSAMA BIN LADEN'S TERRORIST NETWORK

STEVE McBRIDE
Courtesy Independence Daily Reporter (Kan.)

BILL MANGOLD
Courtesy Heritage Newspapers

DICK LOCHER
Courtesy Chicago Tribune

PAUL NOWAK
Courtesy Scripps-Howard News Service

JAMES McCLOSKEY
Courtesy Daily News Leader (Va.)

MARTY RISKIN
Courtesy Georgetown Record (Mass.)

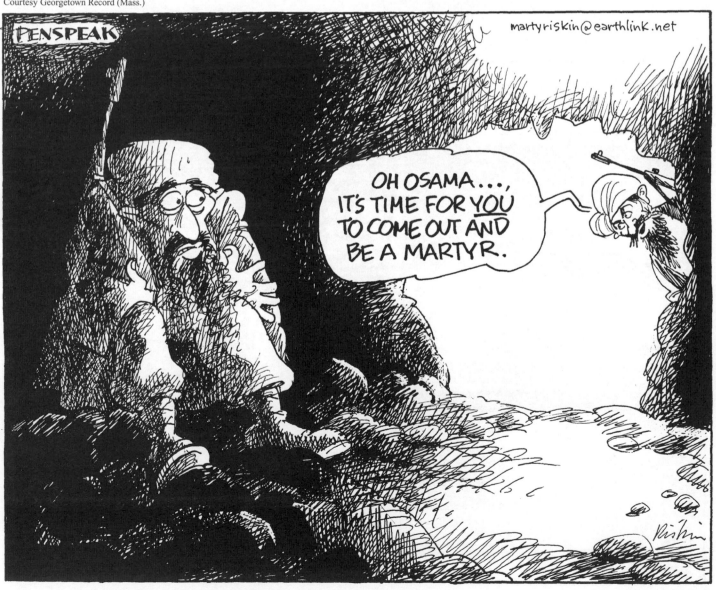

JACK CHAPMAN
Courtesy Desoto Times Today

MIKE THOMPSON
Courtesy Detroit Free Press

WAYNE STAYSKAL
Courtesy Tampa Tribune

KEVIN KALLAUGHER
Courtesy Baltimore Sun

ROBERT ARIAIL
Courtesy The State (S.C.)

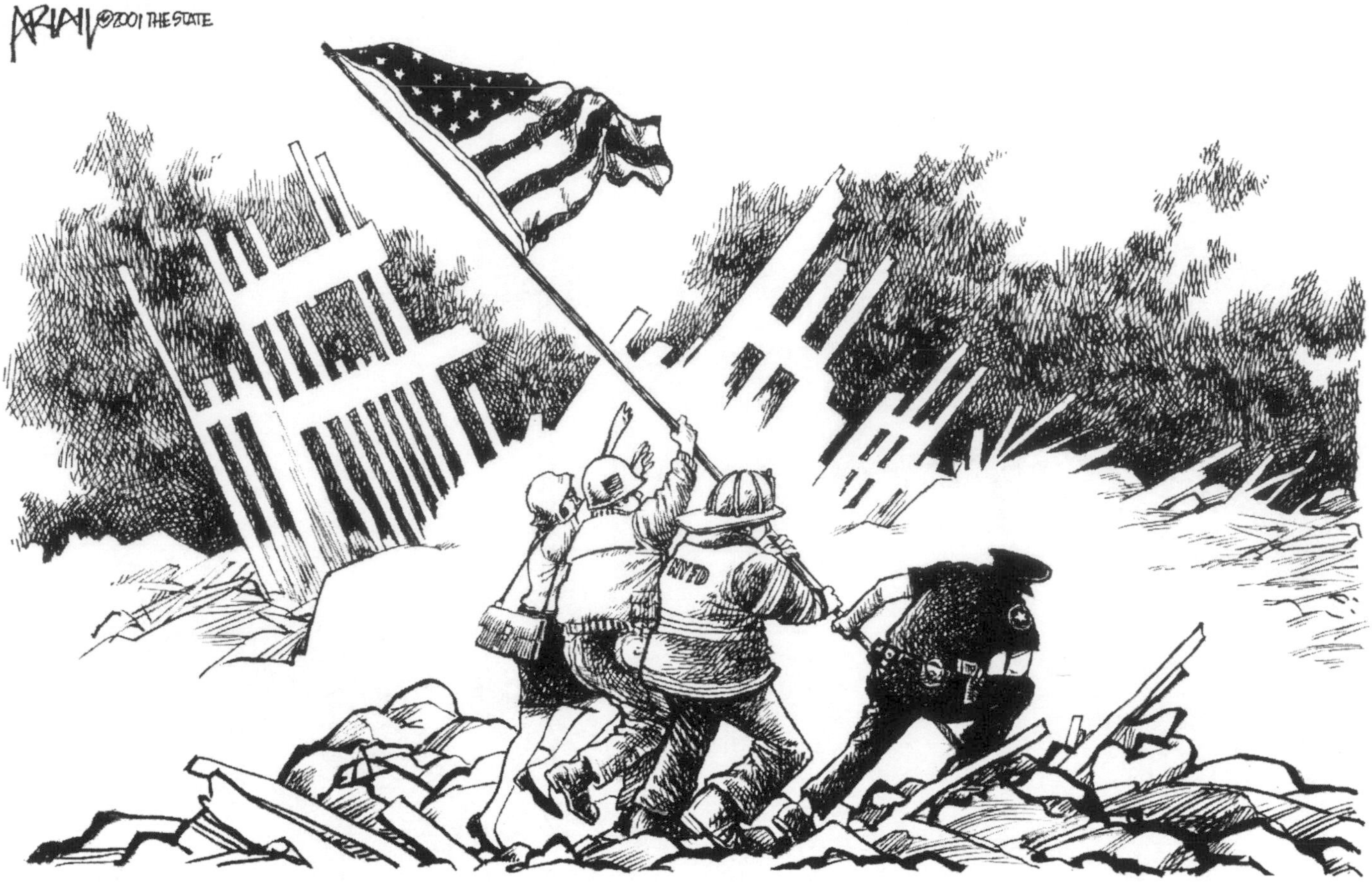
ARIAIL ©2001 THE STATE

DICK LOCHER
Courtesy Chicago Tribune

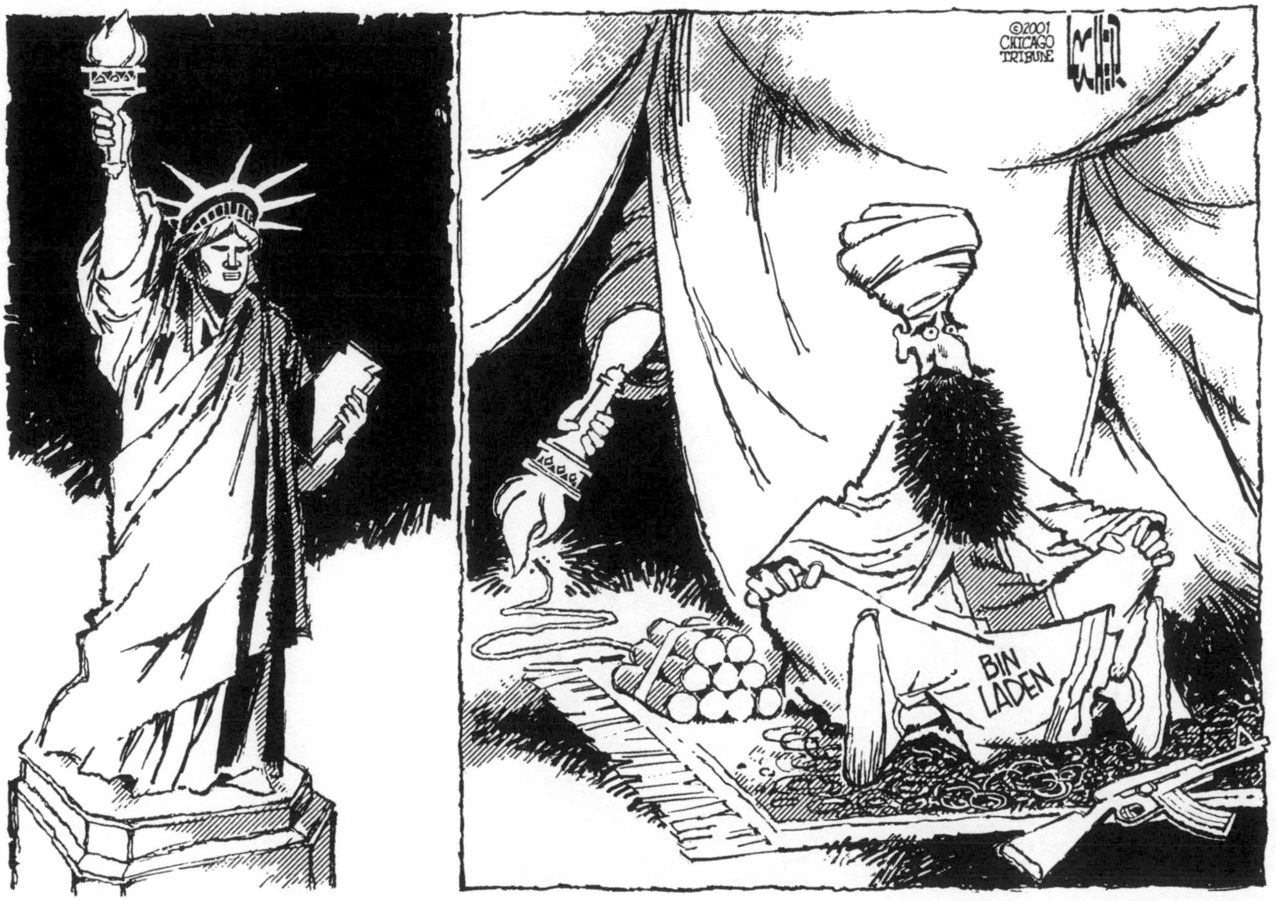
©2001 CHICAGO TRIBUNE
LOCHER
BIN LADEN

A BOOK WITHOUT AN ENDING

STEVE GREENBERG
Courtesy Marin Independent Journal

ED FISCHER
Courtesy Rochester Post-Bulletin

JOHN BRANCH
Courtesy San Antonio Express-News

ROY PETERSON
Courtesy Vancouver Sun

DEAD MAN RUNNING

BOB ENGLEHART
Courtesy Hartford Courant

BRIAN DUFFY
Courtesy Des Moines Register

STUART CARLSON
Courtesy Milwaukee Journal-Sentinel

JOHN SHERFFIUS
Courtesy St. Louis Post-Dispatch

68

STEVEN LAIT
Courtesy Oakland Tribune

JOHN DEERING
Courtesy Arkansas Democrat

PAUL CONRAD
Courtesy Los Angeles Times Syndicate

"READ MY LIPS."

The Bush Administration

Following his narrow victory in the presidential campaign, George W. Bush had hoped for bipartisan cooperation in the early months of his term, but some of his cabinet choices immediately drew stiff opposition. By mid-year, however, Bush was able to deliver on his major campaign promise: a tax cut.

Many Democrats and much of the media felt that the new president lacked the stature—and the brains—to handle the country's top job. Citizens across the country gave him a high grade, however, as he dealt with the problems of a changing world. Polls showed that most voters agreed with his plan to extract more coal and oil in Alaska.

After the September attacks, Bush took a steadfast position: the U.S. was at war and would do whatever it had to do to rid the world of terrorists. His stature grew and his approval rating soared. The international coalition he skillfully assembled—composed of Britain, Russia, Pakistan, Germany, Canada, and other free-world nations—forced the collapse of the Taliban much quicker than most experts had predicted.

As the war escalated, Vice President Dick Cheney was moved out of Washington for security reasons.

THE COALITION

RICK KOLLINGER
Courtesy Easton Star-Democrat

FRANK CAMMUSO
Courtesy Syracuse Herald-Journal

STEVE KELLEY
Courtesy San Diego Union-Tribune

GARY MARKSTEIN
Courtesy Milwaukee Journal Sentinel

MICHAEL RAMIREZ
Courtesy Los Angeles Times

"THE GOOD NEWS IS THAT WE'RE ABOUT TO HAVE
AN ECONOMIC BREAKTHROUGH!"

DEPENDENCE DAY

74

RICHARD CROWSON
Courtesy Wichita Eagle

DAVE GRANLUND
Courtesy Toler Media Services

PAUL CONRAD
Courtesy Los Angeles Times Syndicate

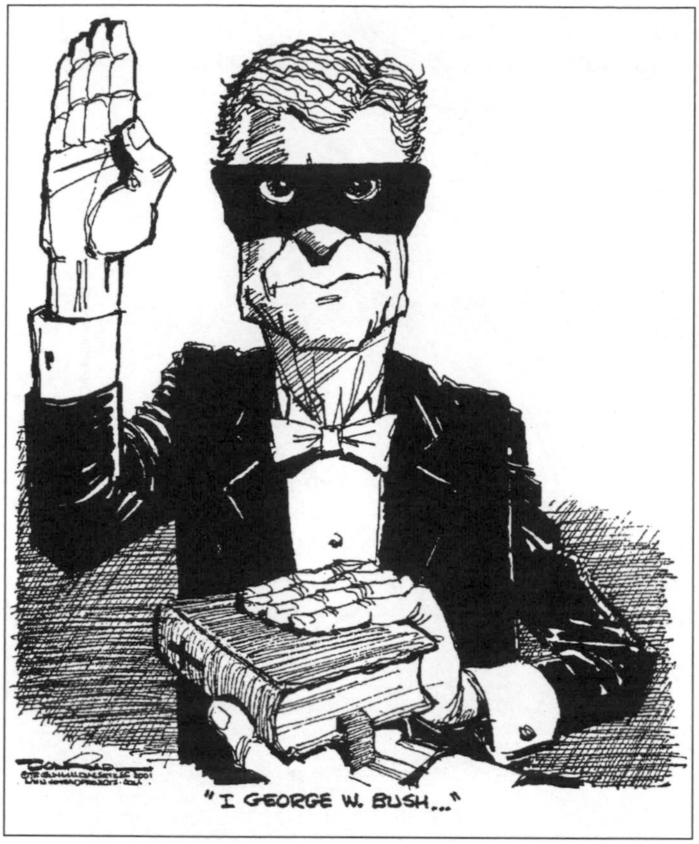
"I GEORGE W. BUSH..."

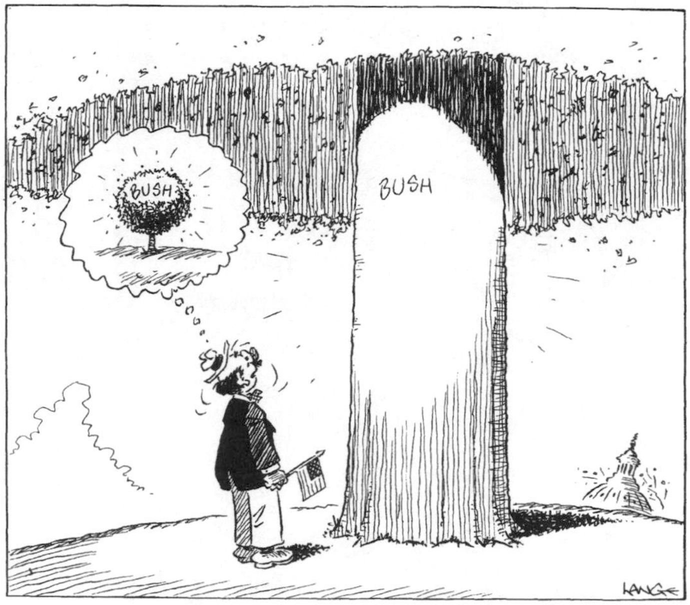
BUSH
BUSH
LANGE

JIM LANGE
Courtesy The Daily Oklahoman

DANA SUMMERS
Courtesy Orlando Sentinel

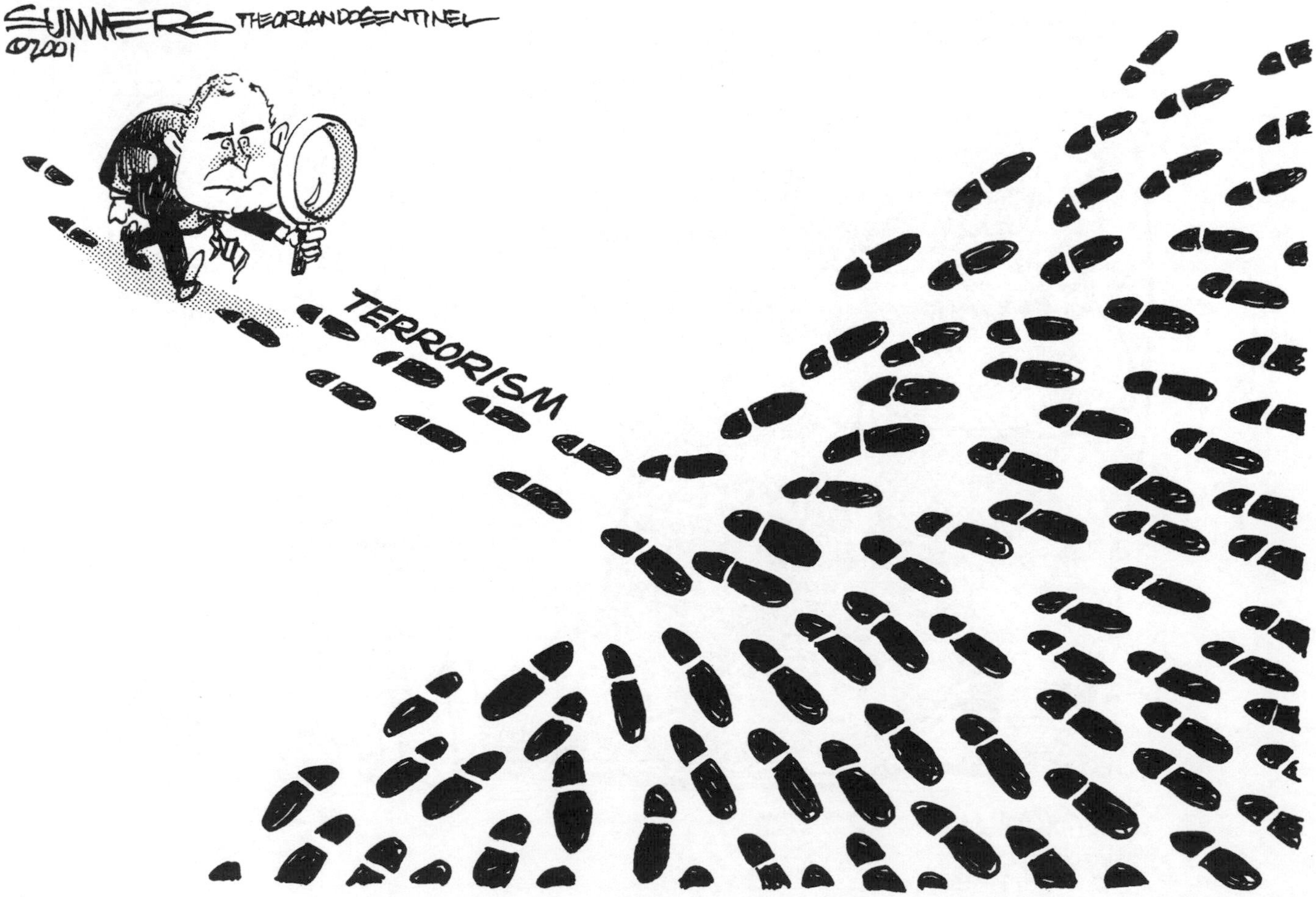
SUMMERS THE ORLANDO SENTINEL
©2001
TERRORISM

CLAY BENNETT
Courtesy Christian Science Monitor

JON RICHARDS
Courtesy Albuquerque Journal North

(This cartoon ran on September 10, the day before the destruction of the Twin Towers in New York City.)

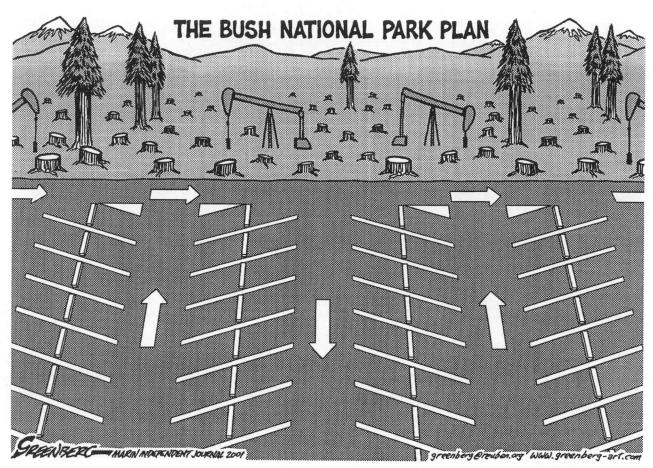

STEVE GREENBERG
Courtesy Marin Independent Journal

MIKE KEEFE
Courtesy Denver Post

GEORGE DANBY
Courtesy Bangor Daily News

MIKE THOMPSON
Courtesy Detroit Free Press

PAUL CONRAD
Courtesy Los Angeles Times Syndicate

AIR FORCE ONE

BRUCE BEATTIE
Courtesy Daytona Beach News-Journal

"It was a palm tree before Bush became president."

ED STEIN
Courtesy Rocky Mountain News

80

CHAN LOWE
Courtesy Fort Lauderdale News/Sun Sentinel

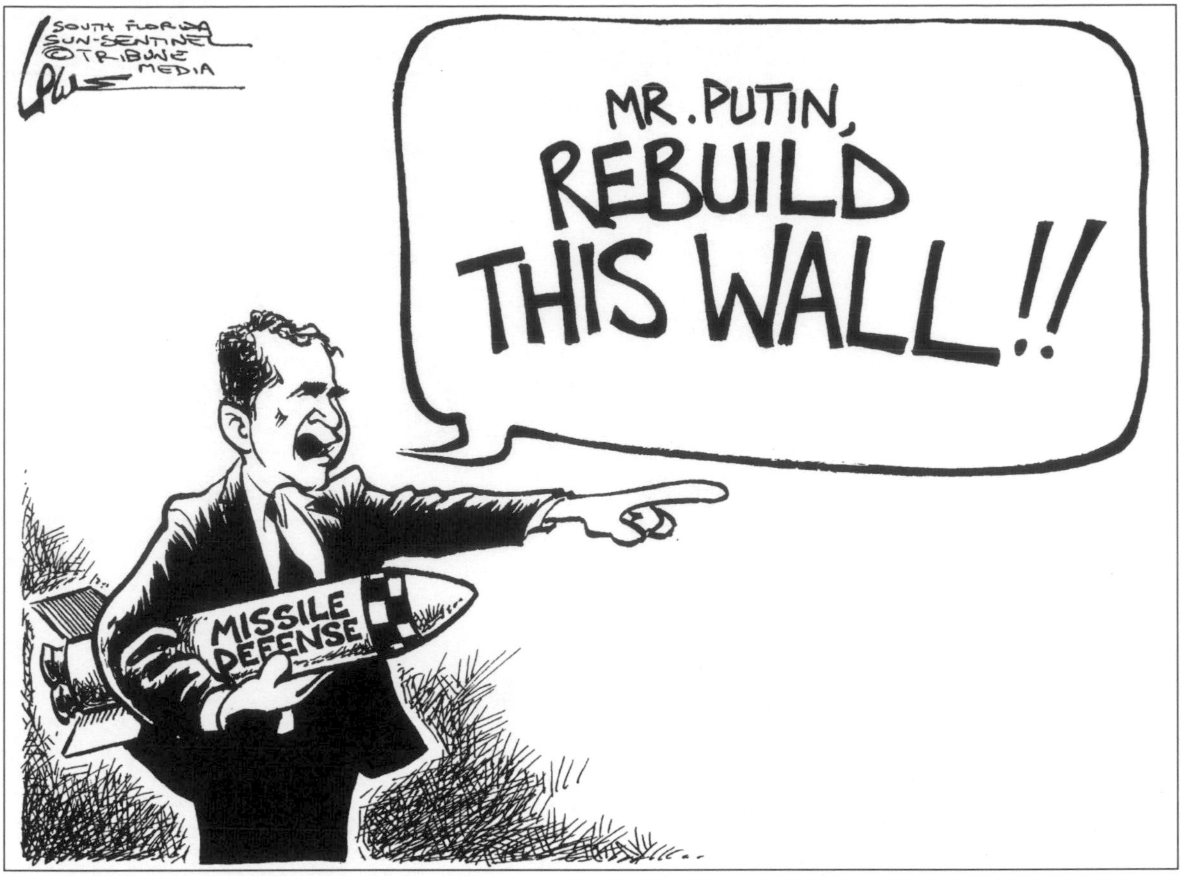
SOUTH FLORIDA SUN-SENTINEL ©TRIBUNE MEDIA
MR. PUTIN, REBUILD THIS WALL!!
MISSILE DEFENSE

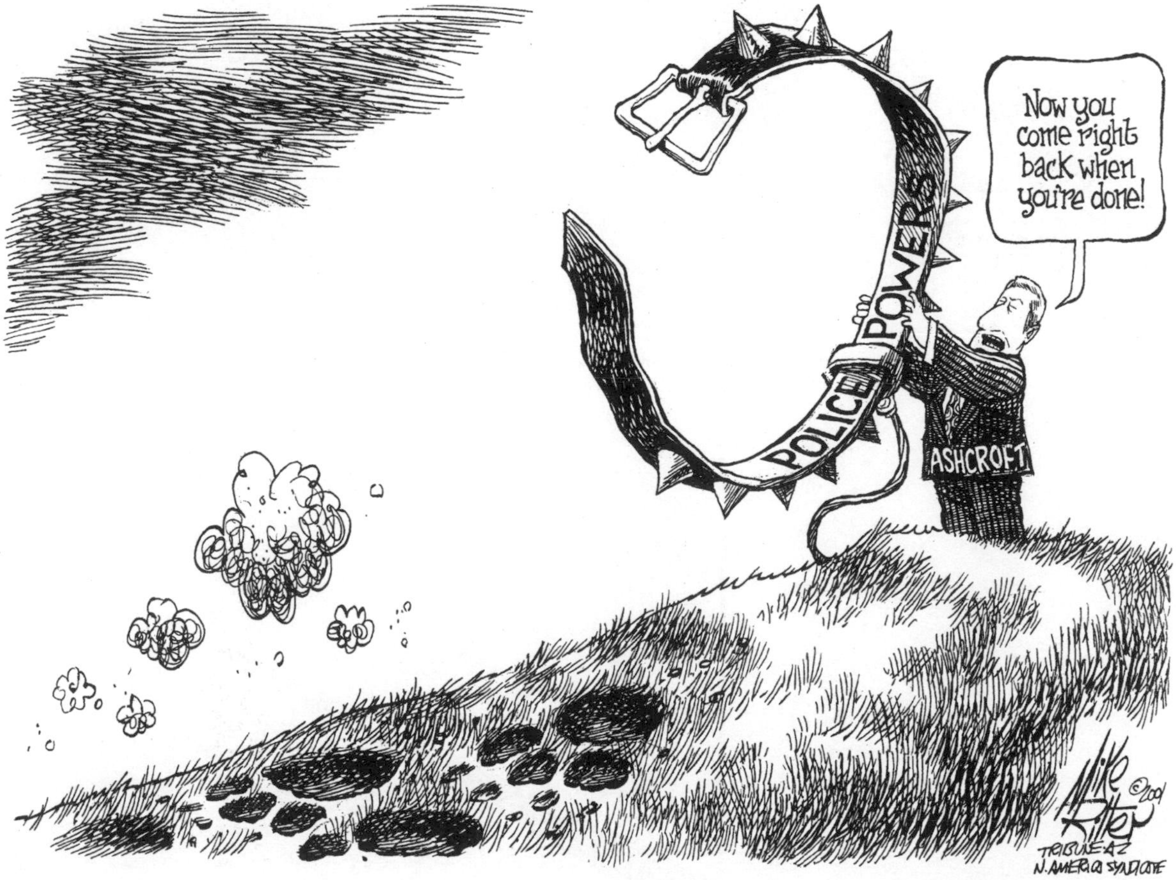
Now you come right back when you're done!
POLICE POWERS
ASHCROFT
©2001
TRIBUNE MEDIA SERVICES
N. AMERICA SYNDICATE

MIKE RITTER
Courtesy Tribune Newspapers

KEN DAVIS
Courtesy Cedartown Standard (Ga.)

MARK STREETER
Courtesy Savannah Morning News

JOHN BRANCH
Courtesy San Antonio Express-News

ANN TELNAES
Courtesy Tribune Media Services

WAYNE STAYSKAL
Courtesy Tampa Tribune

J.R. ROSE
Courtesy Byrd Newspapers

JOEL PETT
Courtesy Lexington Herald-Leader

The Democrats

President Bill Clinton remained a controversial figure in the closing days of his administration. Just before leaving office he issued 150 pardons, including one to his brother, Roger, jailed for selling cocaine, and another to Susan MacDougal, who served time on charges stemming from the Whitewater investigation of the Clintons.

Clinton also pardoned billionaire Marc Rich, who fled to Switzerland after being accused of tax evasion, price rigging, and illegally buying oil from Iran. Rich's ex-wife had donated more than a million dollars to various Democratic causes.

When the Clintons left the White House, they carried with them some $280,000 worth of gifts, prompting the *Washington Post* to pronounce judgment: "They have no capacity for embarrassment."

Jesse Jackson was forced to acknowledge that he had fathered a daughter with a 39-year-old aide. The Baptist minister had acted as spiritual adviser to President Clinton during the Monica Lewinsky scandal. Jackson agreed that what he had done was wrong and asked his followers to forgive him.

Former U.S. Attorney General Janet Reno finally made up her mind about her future, declaring she will run for governor of Florida. She said she would travel the state in her red pickup truck to woo voters.

MIKE PETERS
Courtesy Dayton Daily News

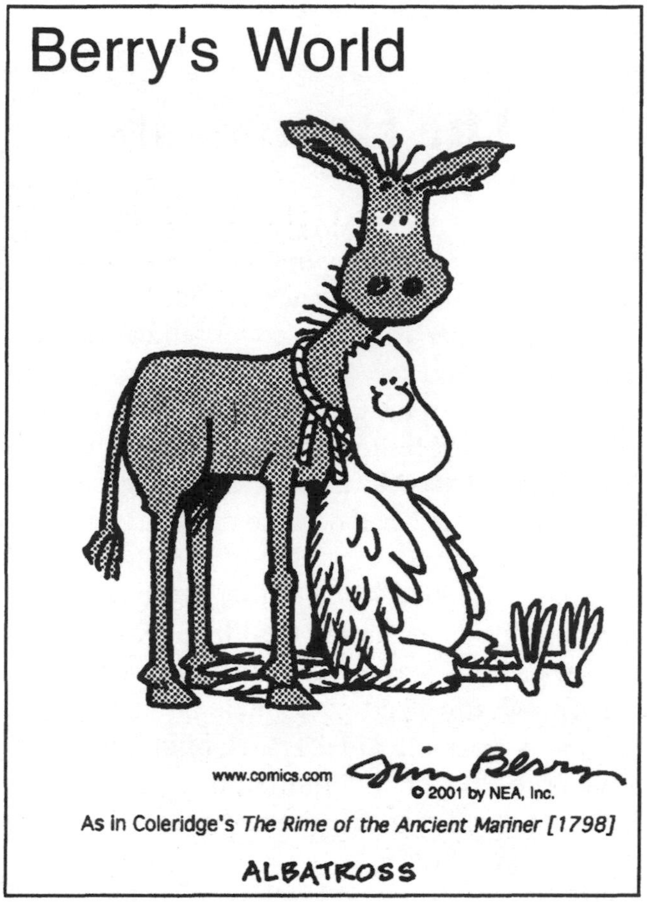
Berry's World
www.comics.com
© 2001 by NEA, Inc.
As in Coleridge's The Rime of the Ancient Mariner [1798]
ALBATROSS

JIM BERRY
Courtesy NEA

SCOTT STANTIS
Courtesy Birmingham News

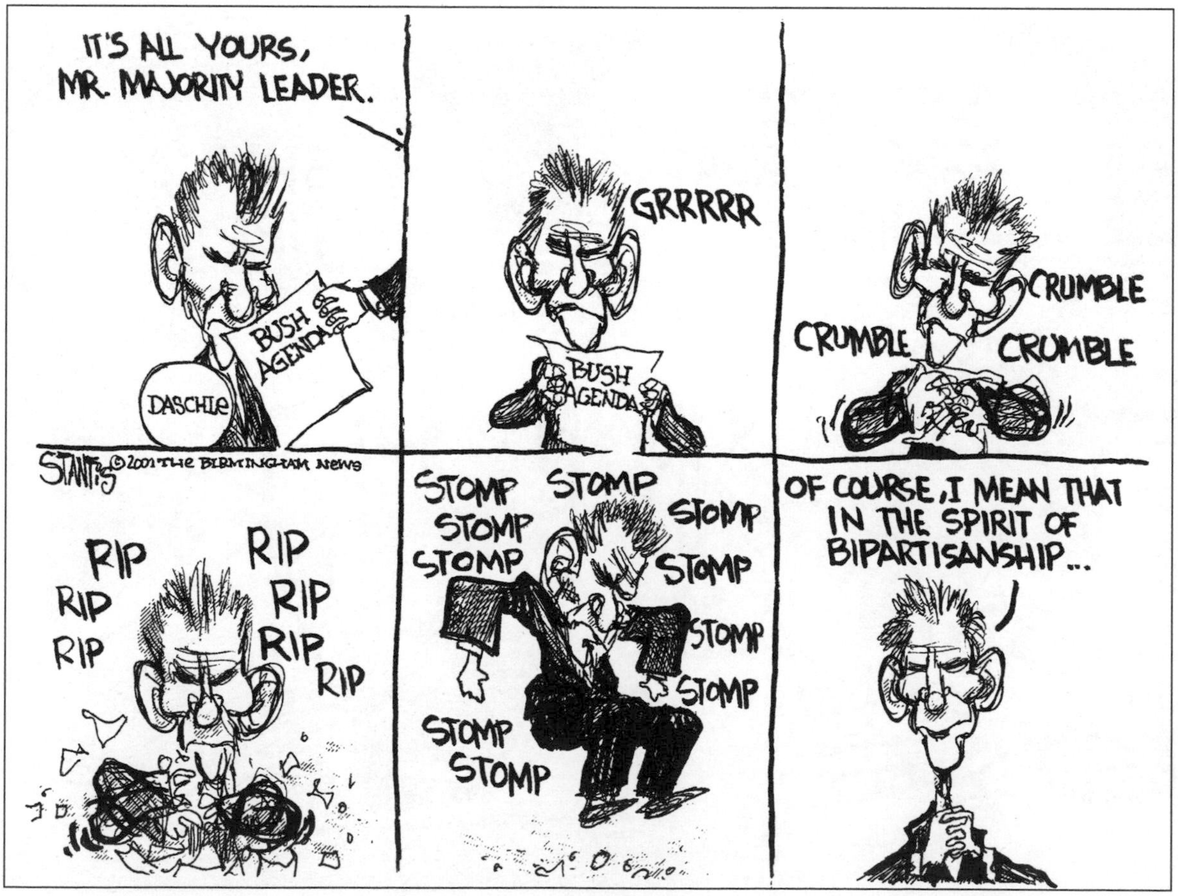
IT'S ALL YOURS, MR. MAJORITY LEADER.
BUSH AGENDA
DASCHLE
GRRRRR
BUSH AGENDA
CRUMBLE
CRUMBLE
CRUMBLE
STANTIS ©2001 THE BIRMINGHAM NEWS
RIP RIP RIP RIP RIP RIP RIP
STOMP STOMP STOMP STOMP STOMP STOMP STOMP STOMP STOMP STOMP
OF COURSE, I MEAN THAT IN THE SPIRIT OF BIPARTISANSHIP...

JERRY HOLBERT
Courtesy Boston Herald

MIKE PETERS
Courtesy Dayton Daily News

RANDY BISH
Courtesy Tribune-Review (Pa.)

DAVID COX
Courtesy Arkansas Democrat-Gazette

LARRY WRIGHT
Courtesy Detroit News

88

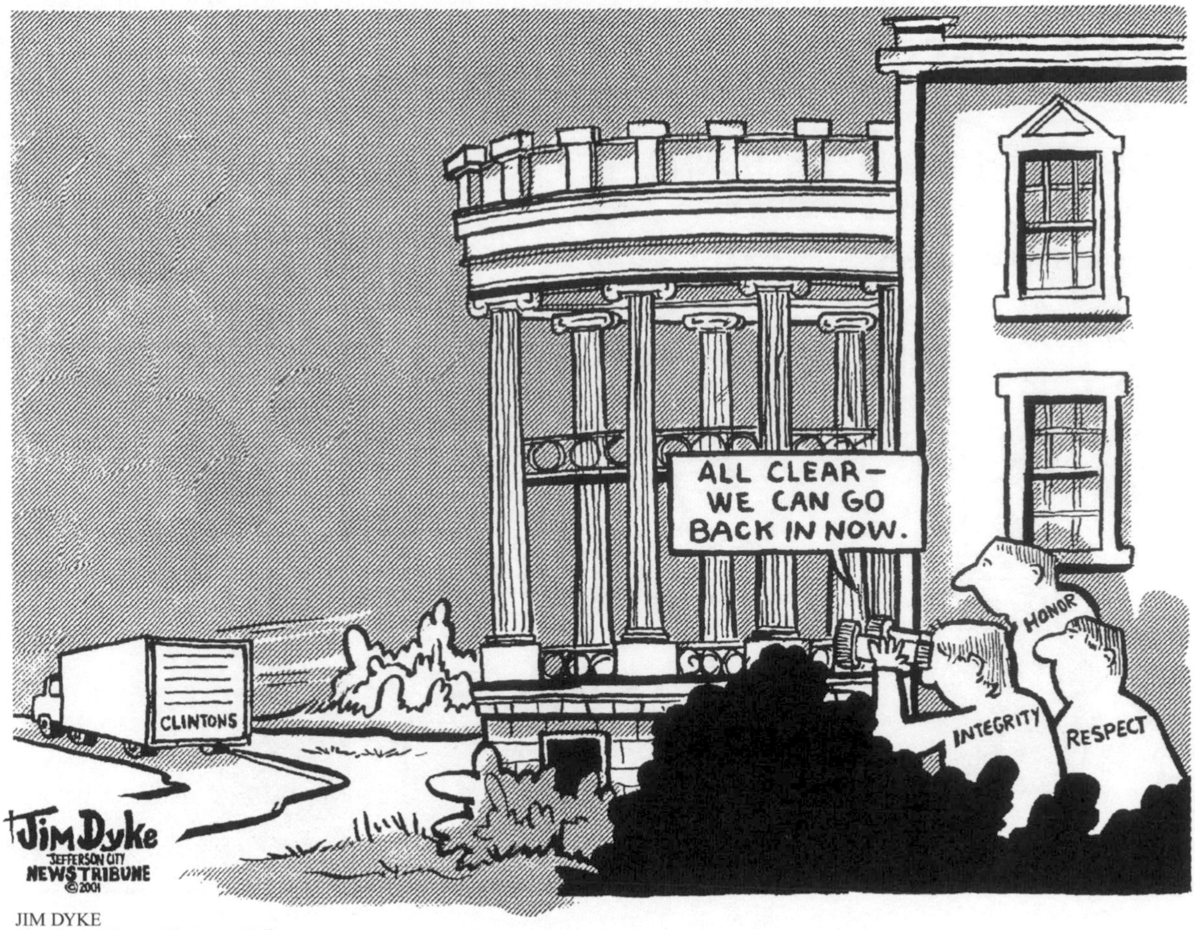
ALL CLEAR—
WE CAN GO
BACK IN NOW.
CLINTONS
HONOR
INTEGRITY
RESPECT
JIM DYKE
JEFFERSON CITY
NEWS TRIBUNE
©2001

JIM DYKE
Courtesy Jefferson City News-Tribune

NEIL GRAHAME
Courtesy Spencer Newspapers

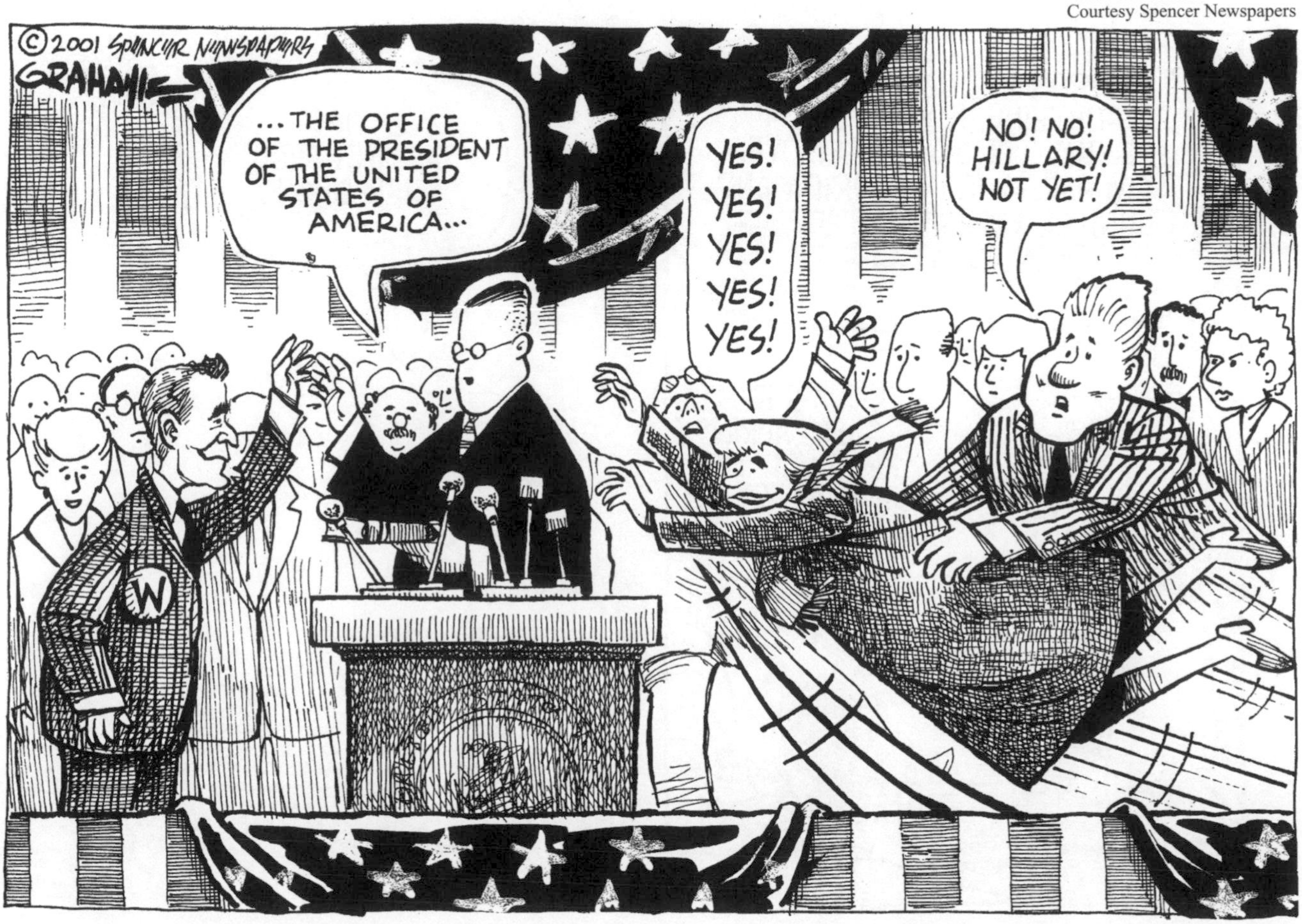
©2001 SPENCER NEWSPAPERS
GRAHAME
...THE OFFICE OF THE PRESIDENT OF THE UNITED STATES OF AMERICA...
YES! YES! YES! YES! YES!
NO! NO! HILLARY! NOT YET!
W

JOHN MARSHALL
Courtesy Binghampton Press and Sun-Bulletin

JEFF PARKER
Courtesy Florida Today

JAKE FULLER
Courtesy Gainesville Sun

RICK KOLLINGER
Courtesy Easton Star-Democrat

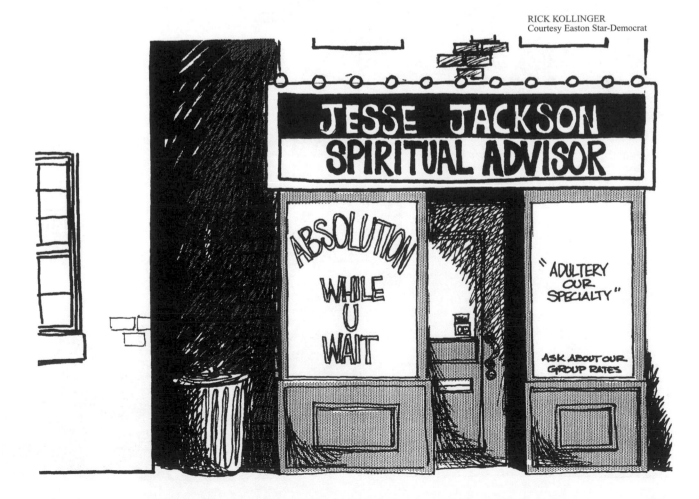

RICKY NOBILE
Courtesy Bolivar Commercial (Miss.)

GARY BROOKINS
Courtesy Richmond Times-Dispatch

ED GAMBLE
Courtesy Florida Times-Union

MICHAEL RAMIREZ
Courtesy Los Angeles Times

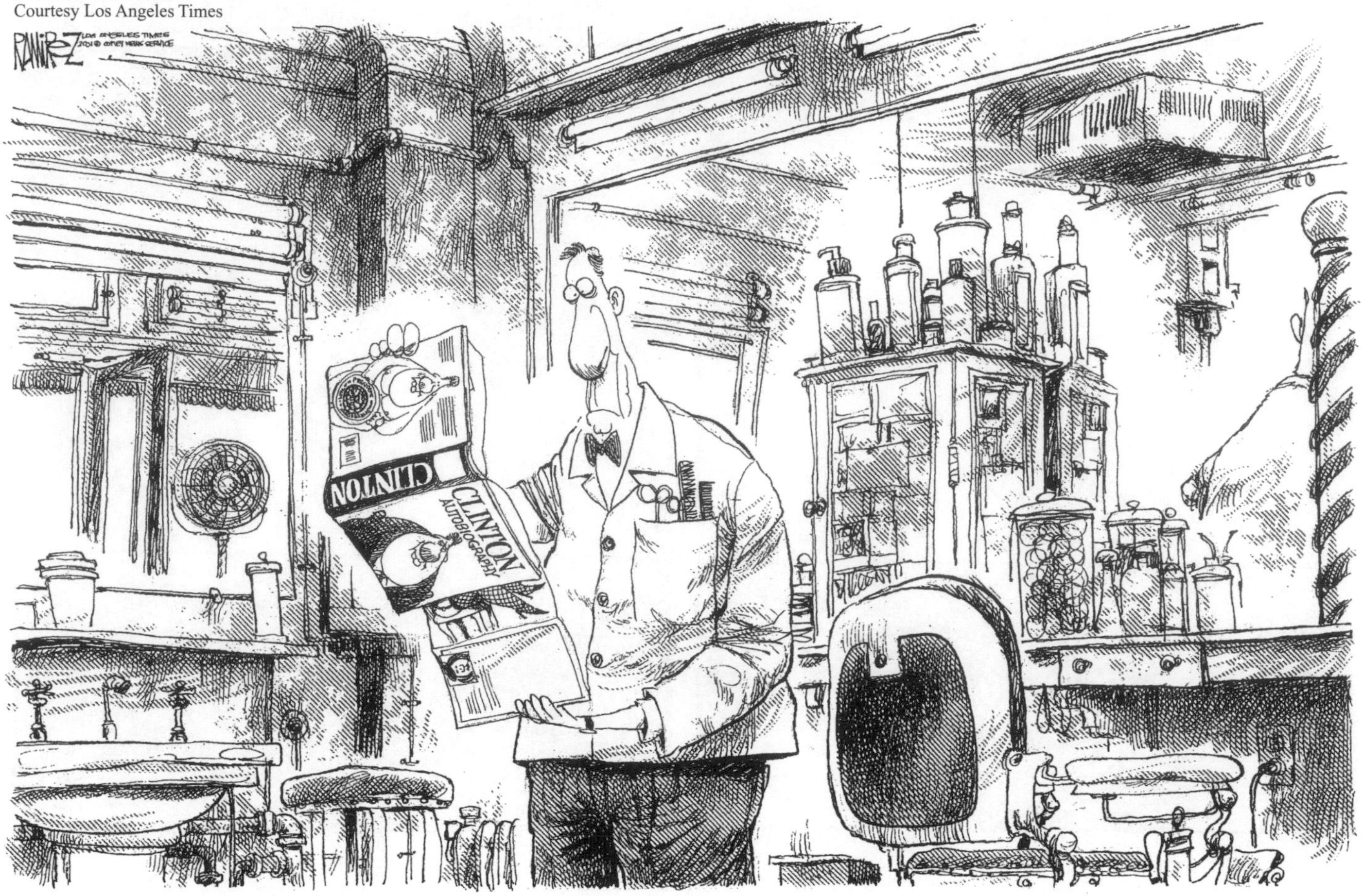
CLINTON
CLINTON AUTOBIOGRAPHY

ROBERT ARIAIL
Courtesy The State (S.C.)

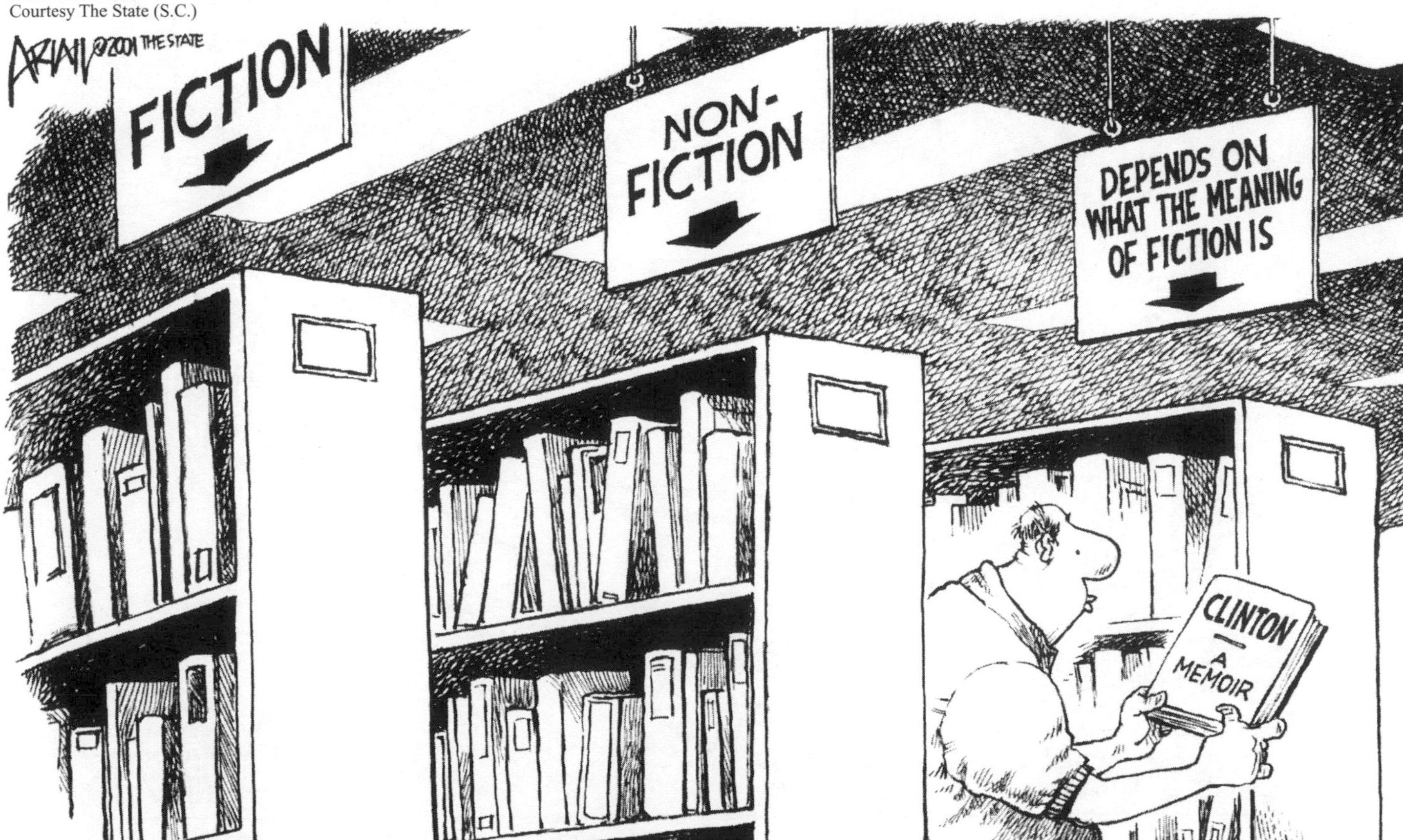
ARIAIL ©2001 THE STATE
FICTION
NON-FICTION
DEPENDS ON WHAT THE MEANING OF FICTION IS
CLINTON
A MEMOIR

WWII

WAR ON TERRORISM

NICK ANDERSON
Courtesy Louisville Courier-Journal

FRANK CAMMUSO
Courtesy Syracuse Herald-Journal

94

The Military

The U.S. attack submarine *Greenville,* in a "one in a billion" accident, struck a Japanese fishing vessel while surfacing off the coast of Hawaii. The fishing boat quickly sank, with the loss of nine lives. Navy officials acknowledged that the accident might have resulted from distractions caused by having fifteen civilians aboard the sub.

The skipper and his radar and sonar technicians had lost track of the 190-foot *Ehima Maru*'s approach. Submarine commander Scott Waddle was removed from command and given a desk job.

Former Nebraska Sen. Bob Kerry announced his regret over an incident dredged up from his service in Viet Nam almost three decades earlier. Kerry had led his team of Navy SEALS in a night engagement against a Viet Cong village. After being fired upon, Kerry said, his group returned fire. They later learned they had killed only women, children, and old men.

The American military demonstrated late in the year that it had adjusted to a completely new kind of war in fighting terrorists. U.S. troops, along with their Northern Alliance allies, were still pursuing remnants of al Queda and Taliban fanatics at year's end.

ROBERT ARIAIL
Courtesy The State (S.C.)

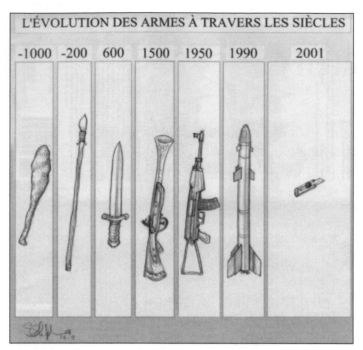

L'ÉVOLUTION DES ARMES À TRAVERS LES SIÈCLES

SERGE CHAPLEAU
Courtesy La Presse (Can.)

JUSTIN DeFREITAS
Courtesy Placerville Mountain Democrat (Calif.)

S.C. RAWLS
Courtesy Rockdale Citizen

96

JAMES CASCIARI
Courtesy Vero Beach Press Journal

JAMES McCLOSKEY
Courtesy Daily News Leader (Va.)

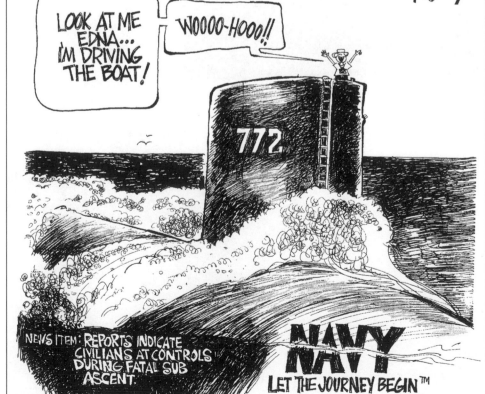

ED STEIN
Courtesy Rocky Mountain News

JOE MAJESKI
Courtesy The Times Leader (Pa.)

KIRK ANDERSON
Courtesy St. Paul Pioneer Press

98

MICHAEL RAMIREZ
Courtesy Los Angeles Times

KERREY
KERREY

YOU KNOW THE NEW RULES— SOMEWHERE OUTSIDE THE RING IS YOUR OPPONENT WITH A STINGER MISSILE...
U.S.
ED FISCHER
© 2001 Rochester Post-Bulletin Co. L.L.C.
Ed Fischer Syndicate
fischer@postbulletin.com

ED FISCHER
Courtesy Rochester Post-Bulletin

EUGENE PAYNE
Courtesy Charlotte Observer

BOB ENGLEHART
Courtesy Hartford Courant

Anthrax and the Media

Two famous names—Senate Majority Leader Tom Daschle and NBC television anchorman Tom Brokaw—received mail in October containing anthrax spores. Both letters bore postmarks from Trenton, New Jersey. The media immediately jumped on the story, magnifying it and in effect terrorizing unnecessarily a great many Americans. For weeks, the anthrax scare was daily front-page news.

Anthrax, of course, can be deadly, but if caught in time it can be treated successfully with antibiotics such as Cipro. Since neither Senator Daschle nor Brokaw personally opened the letters, neither seemed to be at substantial risk. By year's end, just over a dozen Americans had contracted the disease, most of them apparently from cross-contaminated letters, and four people had died.

The Postal Service ordered anthrax testing at 200 mail centers along the East Coast and random testing around the country. The number of people infected remained tiny, but the *Washington Post* was left wondering whether "the U.S. mail stream as a whole at some point might need to be deemed potentially deadly." Most Americans regarded this as over-reaction.

After much study, the FBI concluded that the letters had been sent by a single, homegrown terrorist in the Unabomber mold.

SCOTT STANTIS
Courtesy Birmingham News

MIKE LUCKOVICH
Courtesy Atlanta Constitution

JAKE FULLER
Courtesy Gainesville Sun

MIKE RITTER
Courtesy Tribune Newspapers

BRIAN KELLY
Courtesy Oakland Urbanview

ANN TELNAES
Courtesy Tribune Media Services

BILL YORTH
Courtesy Waukesha Freeman (Wis.)

JACK CHAPMAN
Courtesy Desoto Times Today

WALT HANDELSMAN
Courtesy Newsday

JOHN DEERING
Courtesy Arkansas Democrat

BOB RICH
Courtesy New Haven Register

DAVID REDDICK
Courtesy The Herald Bulletin (Ind.)

MIKE PETERS
Courtesy Dayton Daily News

MICHAEL RAMIREZ
Courtesy Los Angeles Times

107

J.R. ROSE
Courtesy Byrd Newspapers

DANIEL FENECH
Courtesy Saline Reporter

CHUCK ASAY
Courtesy Colorado Springs Gazette-Telegraph

ANN CLEAVES
Courtesy Palisadian Post

TED RALL
Courtesy Universal Press Syndicate

COMPUTER: $1200

INTERNET ACCESS: $30 MONTH

REALIZING YOU CAN'T GET ANTHRAX
FROM E-MAIL: PRICELESS

DON LANDGREN, JR.
Courtesy The Landmark (Mass.)

CHESTER COMMODORE
Courtesy Chicago Defender

JUST OPEN IT! IT'S YOUR SOCIAL **SECURITY** CHECK!

WALT HANDELSMAN
Courtesy Newsday

WAYNE STAYSKAL
Courtesy Tampa Tribune

BILL JANOCHA
Courtesy Greenwich Time

WALT HANDELSMAN
Courtesy Newsday

WALT HANDELSMAN ©2001 Newsday
UNITED STATES POSTAL SERVICE
MAIL

JIM BUSH
Courtesy Providence Journal (R.I.)

U.S. MAIL

TOM GIBB
Courtesy Johnstown Tribune-Democrat (Pa.)

TOM GIBB THE TRIBUNE-DEMOCRAT ©2001
PUBLIC HEALTH OFFICIALS CONFIRMED THAT AFTER OPENING MAIL YESTERDAY, 3,000 AMERICANS TESTED POSITIVE FOR PANIC ATTACKS.

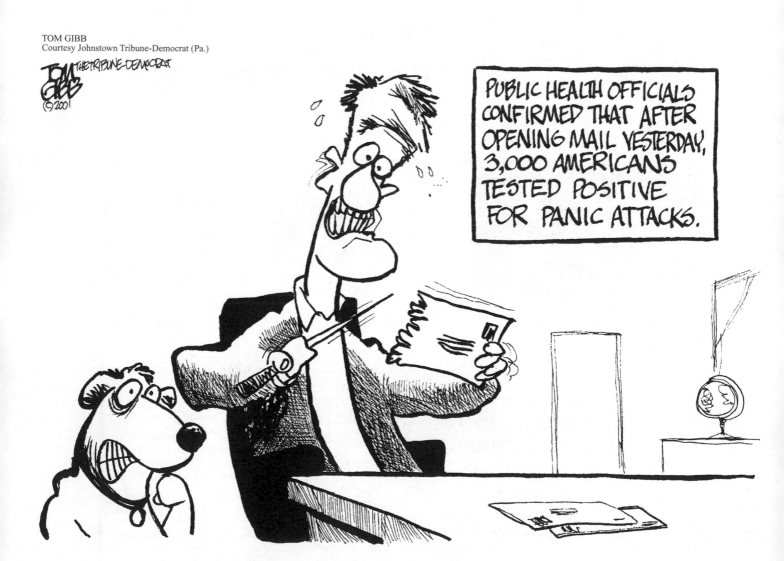

TOM BORROMEO
Courtesy San Francisco Examiner

STACY CURTIS
Courtesy MSNBC & The Times

ED FISCHER
Courtesy Rochester Post-Bulletin

JOE HELLER
Courtesy Green Bay Press-Gazette

The World Economy

The September 11 terrorist attacks helped push the U.S. economy into recession, after the longest economic expansion in the nation's history. Although the economy had begun to slow in the summer of 2000, experts concluded by late 2001 that a full-blown recession had clearly arrived.

In July, an appeals court reversed a lower court order for the breakup of computer giant Microsoft. So, for now, the company has dodged the breakup bullet. The decline of the dot-com industry continued in 2001 to the point that few of those enterprises seemed likely to survive. Chairman Alan Greenspan of the Federal Reserve Board tried to stem the economic slump by repeatedly cutting interest rates.

Gasoline prices went through the roof during the summer, rising to more than two dollars a gallon in many areas. But by the end of the year pump prices had plummeted, dropping to below a dollar a gallon.

Companies large and small continued to downsize during 2001. Layoffs were becoming a problem in many industries, and unemployment began to rise.

California continued to wrestle with the problem of providing for its energy needs. The state has not built a power plant in ten years and has been purchasing high-priced electricity from outside the state.

TOMMY THOMPSON
Courtesy San Diego Union-Tribune

ROGER SCHILLERSTROM
Courtesy Crain Communications

RICK TUMA
Courtesy Chicago Tribune

ED HALL
Courtesy Baker County Press

JOEL PETT
Courtesy Lexington Herald-Leader

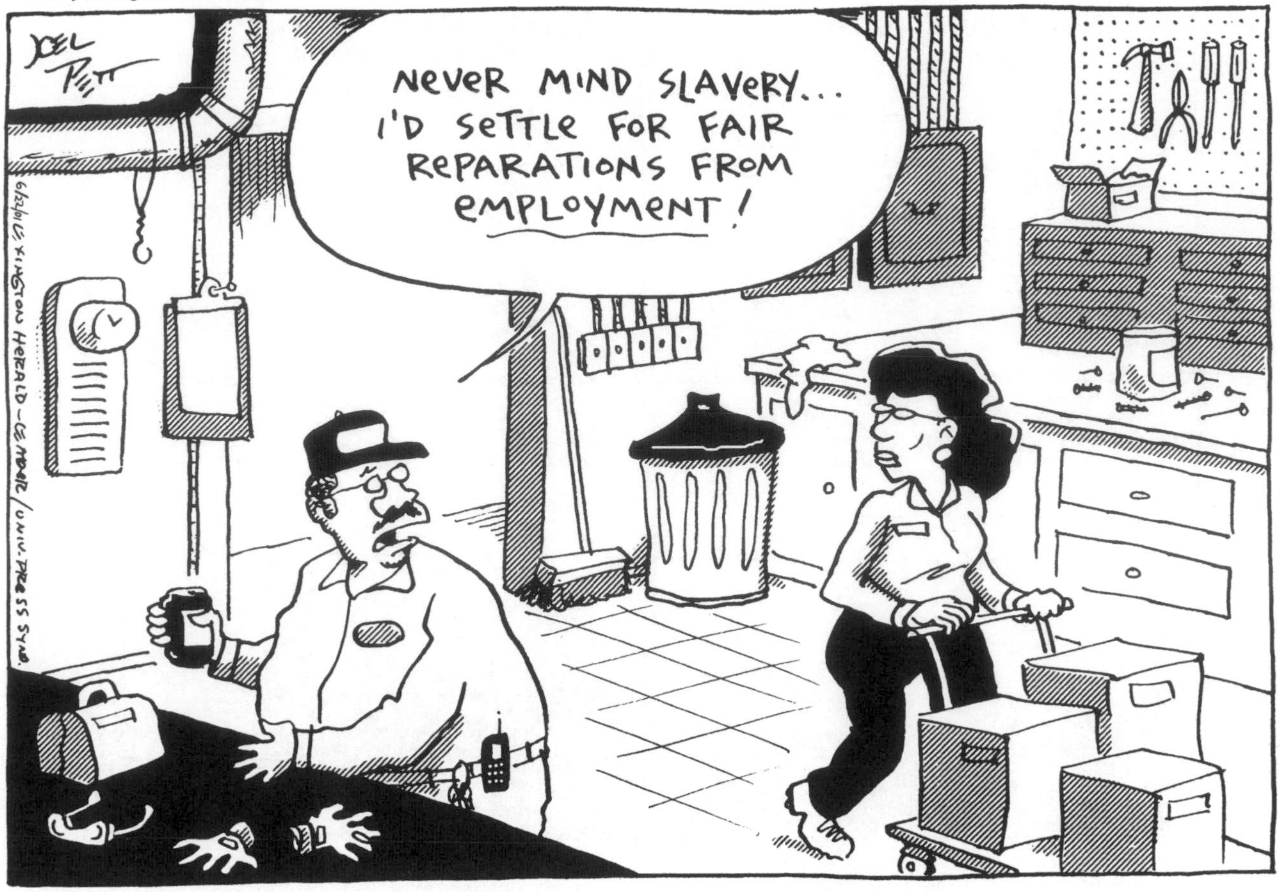
JOEL PETT
NEVER MIND SLAVERY...
I'D SETTLE FOR FAIR
REPARATIONS FROM
EMPLOYMENT!

ROBERT ARIAIL
Courtesy The State (S.C.)

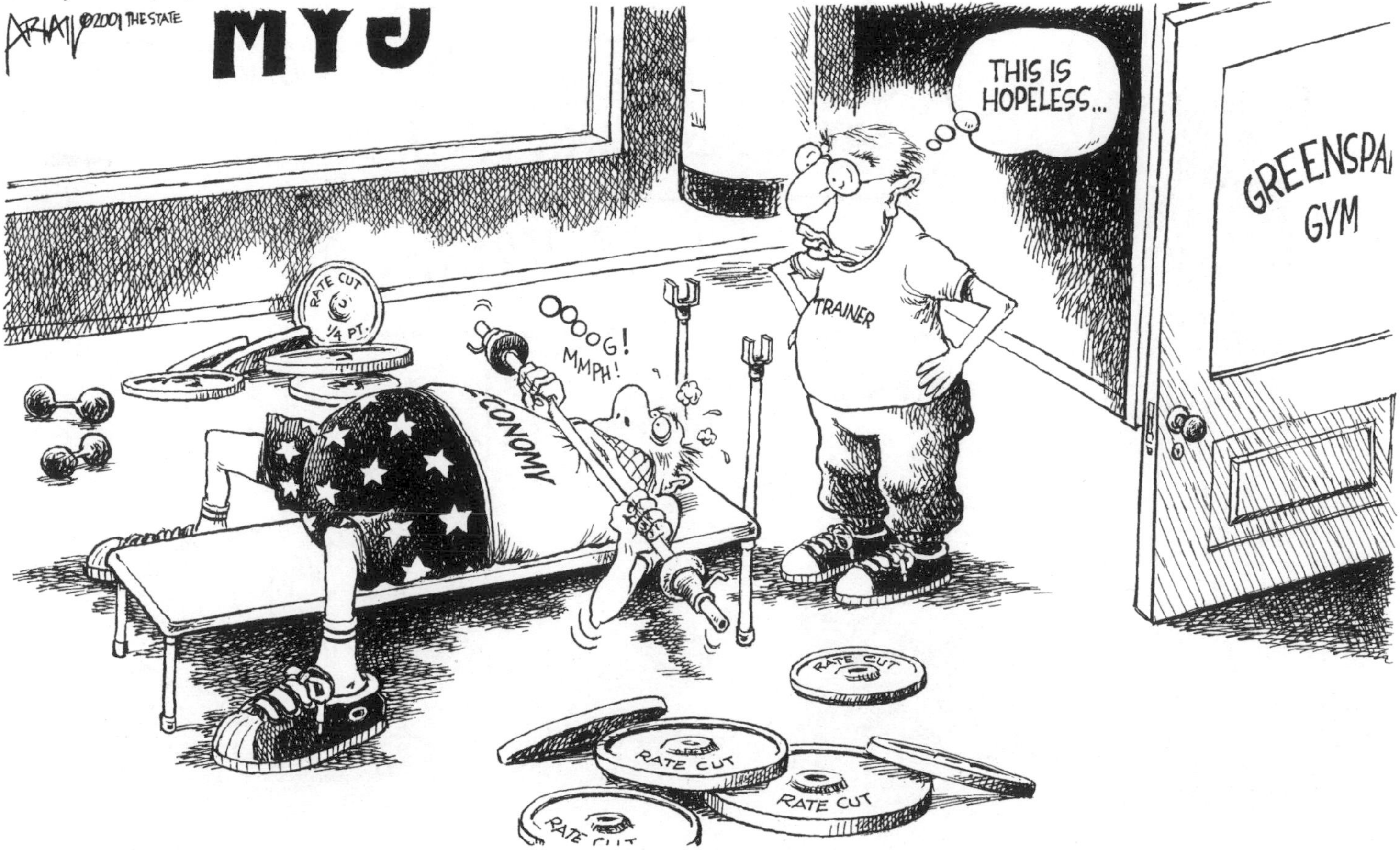
ARIAIL ©2001 THE STATE
MYG
THIS IS HOPELESS...
GREENSPA
GYM
TRAINER
RATE CUT
1/4 PT.
OOOOOG!
MMPH!
ECONOMY
RATE CUT
RATE CUT
RATE CUT

GARY MARKSTEIN
Courtesy Milwaukee Journal Sentinel

FRED MULHEARN
Courtesy The Advocate (La.)

118

KEVIN KALLAUGHER
Courtesy Baltimore Sun

DICK LOCHER
Courtesy Chicago Tribune

119

JERRY BARNETT
Courtesy Indianapolis Star

J.D. CROWE
Courtesy Mobile Register

JIM BORGMAN
Courtesy Cincinnati Enquirer

"CONSUMER CONFIDENCE CRISIS IN AISLE THREE!"

BRIAN DUFFY
Courtesy Des Moines Register

TOM GIBB
Courtesy Johnstown Tribune-Democrat (Pa.)

FRED CURATOLO
Courtesy Edmonton Sun (Can.)

RICHARD WALLMEYER
Courtesy Long Beach Press-Telegram

ROGER SCHILLERSTROM
Courtesy Crain Communications

STEVE McBRIDE
Courtesy Independence Daily Reporter (Kan.)

EUGENE PAYNE
Courtesy Charlotte Observer

DON LANDGREN, JR.
Courtesy The Landmark (Mass.)

JOE HOFFECKER
Courtesy Cincinnati Business Courier

ED GAMBLE
Courtesy Florida Times-Union

CLAY JONES
Courtesy Free Lance Star (Va.)

JACK HIGGINS
Courtesy Chicago Sun-Times

solving California's electricity crisis

RUSSELL HODIN
Courtesy New Times (Calif.)

STEVE LINDSTROM
Courtesy Duluth News-Tribune

KEN DAVIS
Courtesy Cedartown Standard (Ga.)

ED FISCHER
Courtesy Rochester Post-Bulletin

JEFFREY SMITH
Courtesy Kansas City Star

BRUMSIC BRANDON, JR.
Courtesy Florida Today

WILLIAM L. FLINT
Courtesy Arlington Morning News (Tex.)

STUART CARLSON
Courtesy Milwaukee Journal-Sentinel

ANN CLEAVES
Courtesy Palisadian Post

JOHN AUCHTER
Courtesy Grand Rapids Business Journal

ED STEIN
Courtesy Rocky Mountain News

DAVID HITCH
Courtesy Worcester Telegram and Gazette

DAVE SATTLER
Courtesy Lafayette Journal and Courier

VIC CANTONE
Courtesy Brooklyn Paper Publications

ELENA STEIER
Courtesy The Valley News (Conn.)

©2001 Elena Steier

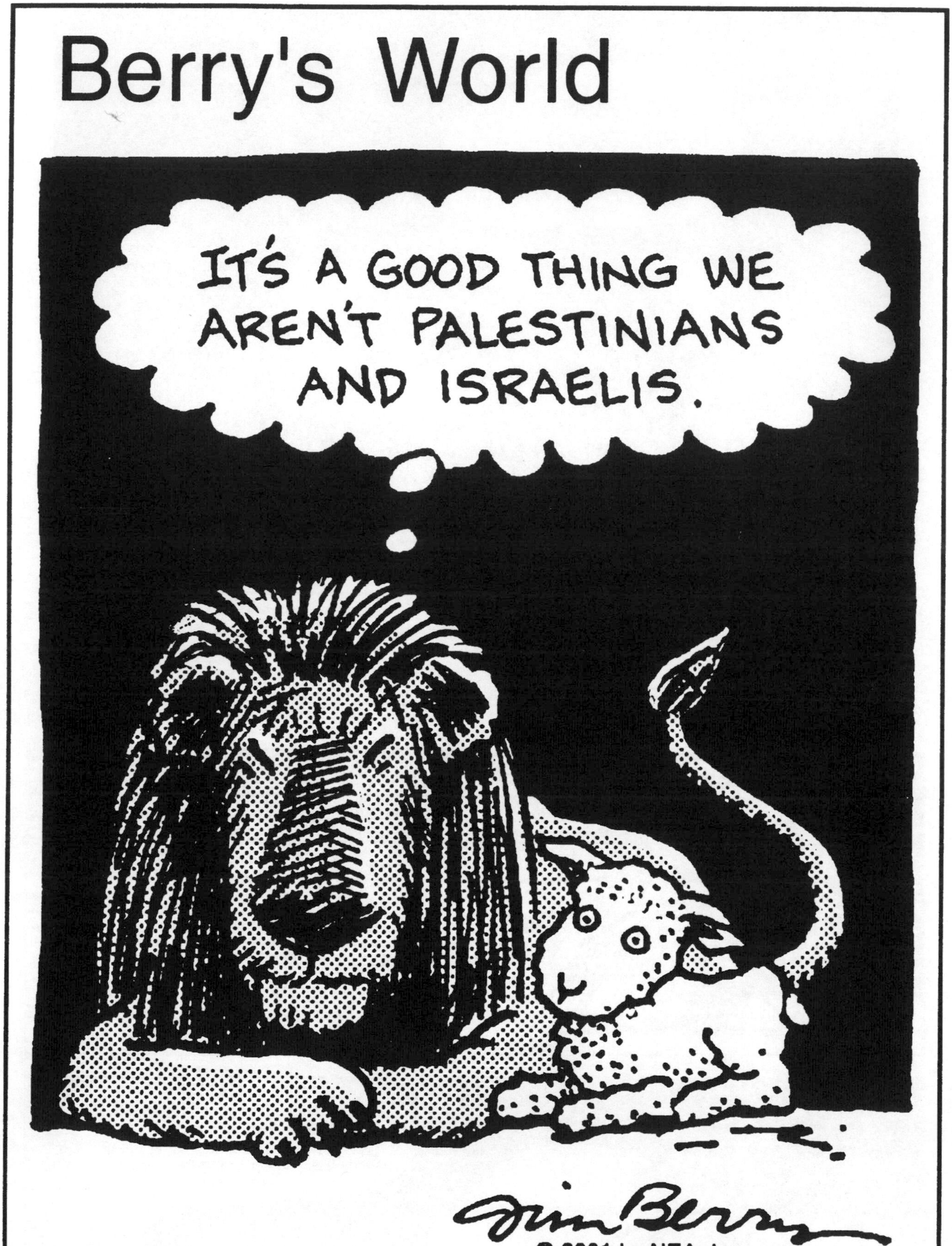
Berry's World
IT'S A GOOD THING WE AREN'T PALESTINIANS AND ISRAELIS.
Jim Berry
© 2001 by NEA, Inc.
www.comics.com

JIM BERRY
Courtesy NEA

Foreign Affairs

Special forces police in Yugoslavia arrested former president Slobodan Milosevic on a variety of charges linked to his decade of repressive rule. Dutch police escorted him to his new home, a prison cell in The Hague. He is expected to be charged with war crimes, but it will likely be at least a year before the trial begins.

Former Israeli general Ariel Sharon won a landslide victory for prime minister against incumbent Ehud Barak. Palestinians, who distrust the conservative Sharon, made good on threats to increase the level of violence.

A Chinese jet fighter collided with a U.S. reconnaissance plane off the coast of China. The Chinese plane crashed, and the crippled American aircraft managed to fly on to a Chinese island, where it safely landed. The Chinese blamed the U.S. for the incident, detained the American crew, and demanded an apology. After eleven days of high-level haggling, the crew was released when Secretary of State Colin Powell announced that the U.S. was "very sorry" the Chinese pilot had lost his life.

Peaceniks and peace-not-war groups demonstrated against U.S. retaliation for the Twin Towers and Pentagon attacks, but the country remained solidly behind President Bush in his handling of the war. The Taliban's cruel treatment of Afghan citizens, particularly women, turned world opinion strongly against the repressive regime.

GARY BROOKINS
Courtesy Richmond Times-Dispatch

TOM BORROMEO
Courtesy San Francisco Examiner

MICHAEL OSBUN
Courtesy Citrus City Chronicle (Fla.)

JOHN TREVER
Courtesy Albuquerque Journal

RICK McKEE
Courtesy Augusta Chronicle (Ga.)

"THE CHINESE ARE HOPPING MAD, SIR. THEY WANT a PUBLIC APOLOGY; THEY WANT US to STOP RECONNAISSANCE FLIGHTS NEAR the CHINESE COAST and THEY WANT CLINTON to RETURN ALL THEIR CAMPAIGN CONTRIBUTIONS...."

SCOTT STANTIS
Courtesy Birmingham News

WE'RE SORRY CHINA'S A TOTALITARIAN, HUMAN RIGHTS CRUSHING, BELLIGERENT, BACKWARDS, PARIAH NATION.

NOT EXACTLY THE APOLOGY WE WERE HOPING FOR....

STUART CARLSON
Courtesy Milwaukee Journal-Sentinel

DREW SHENEMAN
Courtesy Newark Star-Ledger

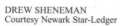

JOHN TREVER
Courtesy Albuquerque Journal

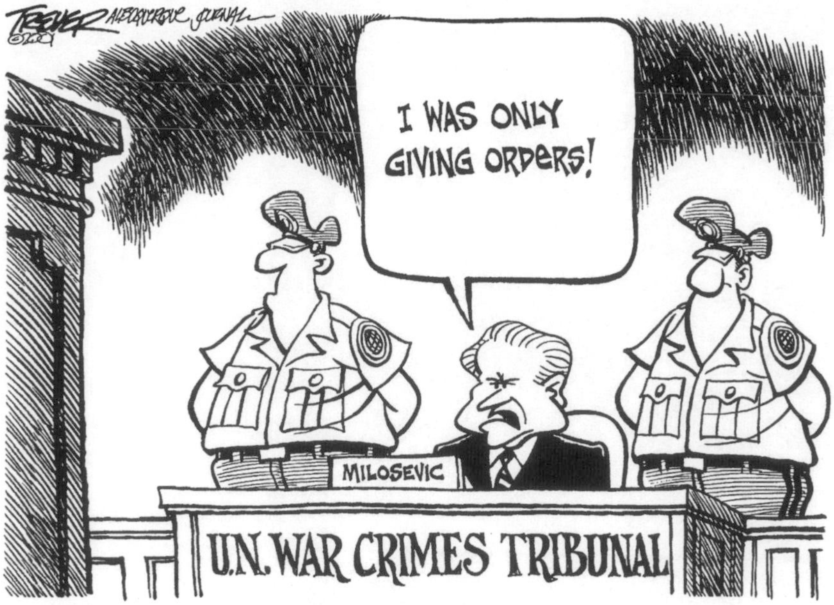
I WAS ONLY GIVING ORDERS!
MILOSEVIC
U.N. WAR CRIMES TRIBUNAL

DENNIS DRAUGHON
Courtesy Scranton Times

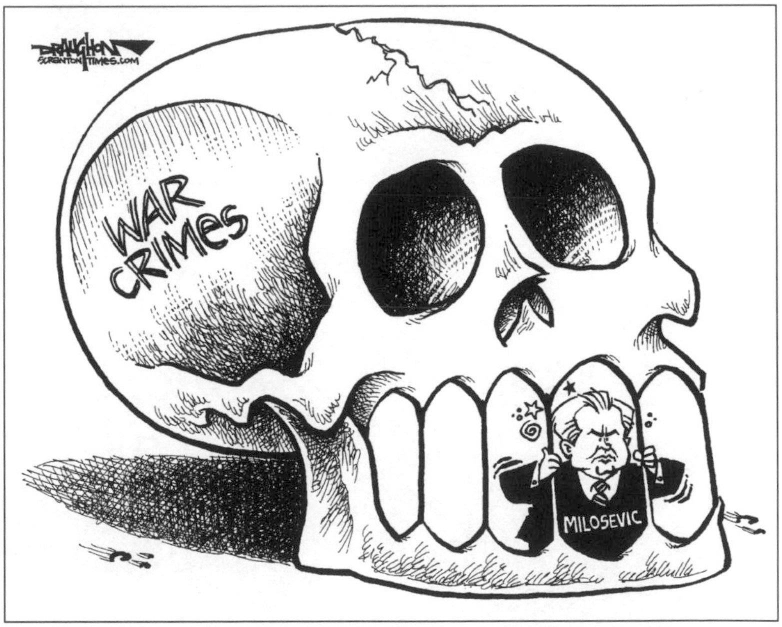
WAR CRIMES
MILOSEVIC

NEIL GRAHAME
Courtesy Spencer Newspapers

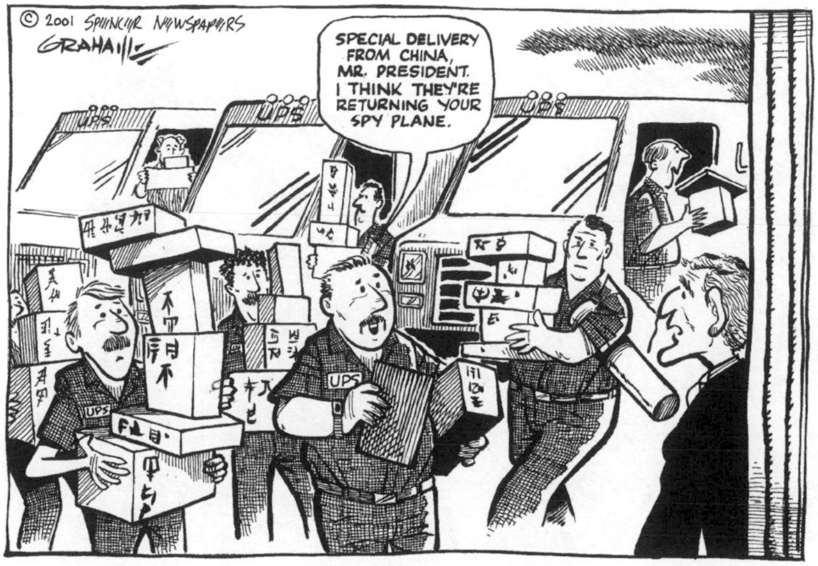
© 2001 SPENCER NEWSPAPERS
SPECIAL DELIVERY FROM CHINA, MR. PRESIDENT. I THINK THEY'RE RETURNING YOUR SPY PLANE.

SERGE CHAPLEAU
Courtesy La Presse (Can.)

MIKE LUCKOVICH
Courtesy Atlanta Constitution

BRUCE BEATTIE
Courtesy Daytona Beach News-Journal

RICK TUMA
Courtesy Chicago Tribune

WALT HANDELSMAN
Courtesy Newsday

CHARLOS GARY
Courtesy Chicago Tribune & DBR Media

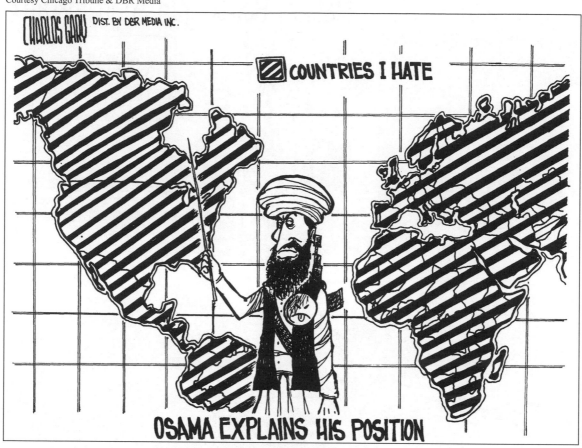

EUGENE PAYNE
Courtesy Charlotte Observer

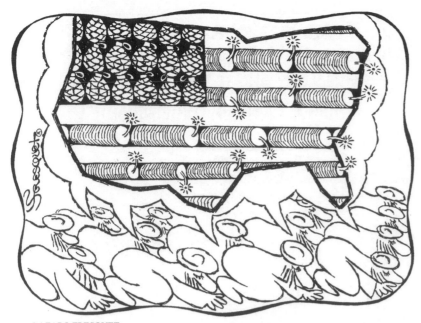

LAZARO FRESQUET
Courtesy El Nuevo Herald (Fla.)

PAUL FELL
Courtesy Lincoln Journal Star (Neb.)

JIMMY MARGULIES
Courtesy The Record (N.J.)

JOHN TREVER
Courtesy Albuquerque Journal

JOHN BRANCH
Courtesy San Antonio Express-News

Congress

Sen. James Jeffords, a Republican from Vermont, set Washington on its ear by announcing that he was leaving the GOP to become an Independent. The defection took control of the Senate from the Republicans and gave it to the Democrats. Instead of being evenly divided 50-50, the Senate was now composed of 50 Democrats, 49 Republicans, and 1 Independent.

When the anthrax scare arose after a staffer in the office of Sen. Tom Daschle opened a letter laced with anthrax spores, the Senate remained open but the House of Representatives completely shut down. Terrorism had thus accomplished what even the Civil War could not—halt the legislative arm of the U.S. government.

The disappearance of former intern Chandra Levy drew nationwide attention due to her rumored relationship with California congressman Gary Condit. Levy has not been seen since she disappeared April 30.

Three durable conservative senators—99-year-old Strom Thurmond of South Carolina, Jesse Helms of North Carolina, and Phil Gramm of Texas—announced their retirement. Several congressmen were alleged to have leaked military secrets, and President Bush drastically reduced the number of lawmakers who had access to such information. As usual, nothing was done about campaign finance reform.

ETTA HULME
Courtesy Fort Worth Star-Telegram

HENRY McCLURE
Courtesy Lawton Constitution

TIM HARTMAN
Courtesy Valley News Dispatch (Pa.)

TERRORISM...

COUNTER-TERRORISM...

DENNIS DRAUGHON
Courtesy Scranton Times

JOHN WEISS
Courtesy Santa Cruz Sentinel

OUR FAVORITE SITCOM WAS INTERRUPTED FOR ANOTHER CHANDRA LEVY NEWS BRIEF, AND POOR FRED HERE KIND OF LOST IT...

ED HALL
Courtesy Baker County Press

JAKE FULLER
Courtesy Gainesville Sun

146

JOE HELLER
Courtesy Green Bay Press-Gazette

STEVEN LAIT
Courtesy Oakland Tribune

JIM BORGMAN
Courtesy Cincinnati Enquirer

DAVID HITCH
Courtesy Worcester Telegram and Gazette

CHUCK ASAY
Courtesy Colorado Springs Gazette-Telegraph

GARY BROOKINS
Courtesy Richmond Times-Dispatch

ANN TELNAES
Courtesy Tribune Media Services

JOSEPH F. O'MAHONEY
Courtesy The Patriot Ledger (Mass.)

SCOTT STANTIS
Courtesy Birmingham News

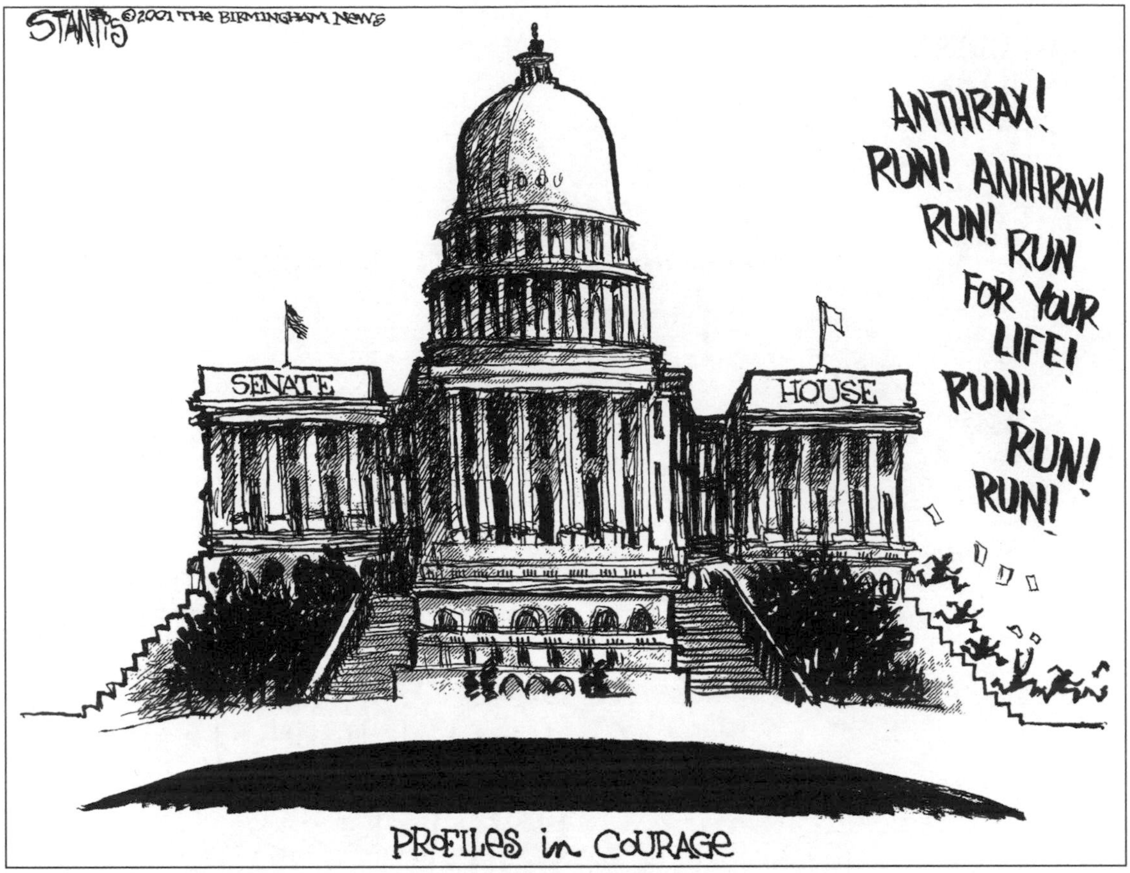
STANTIS ©2001 THE BIRMINGHAM NEWS
SENATE
HOUSE
ANTHRAX!
RUN! ANTHRAX!
RUN! RUN
FOR YOUR
LIFE!
RUN!
RUN!
RUN!
PROFILES in COURAGE

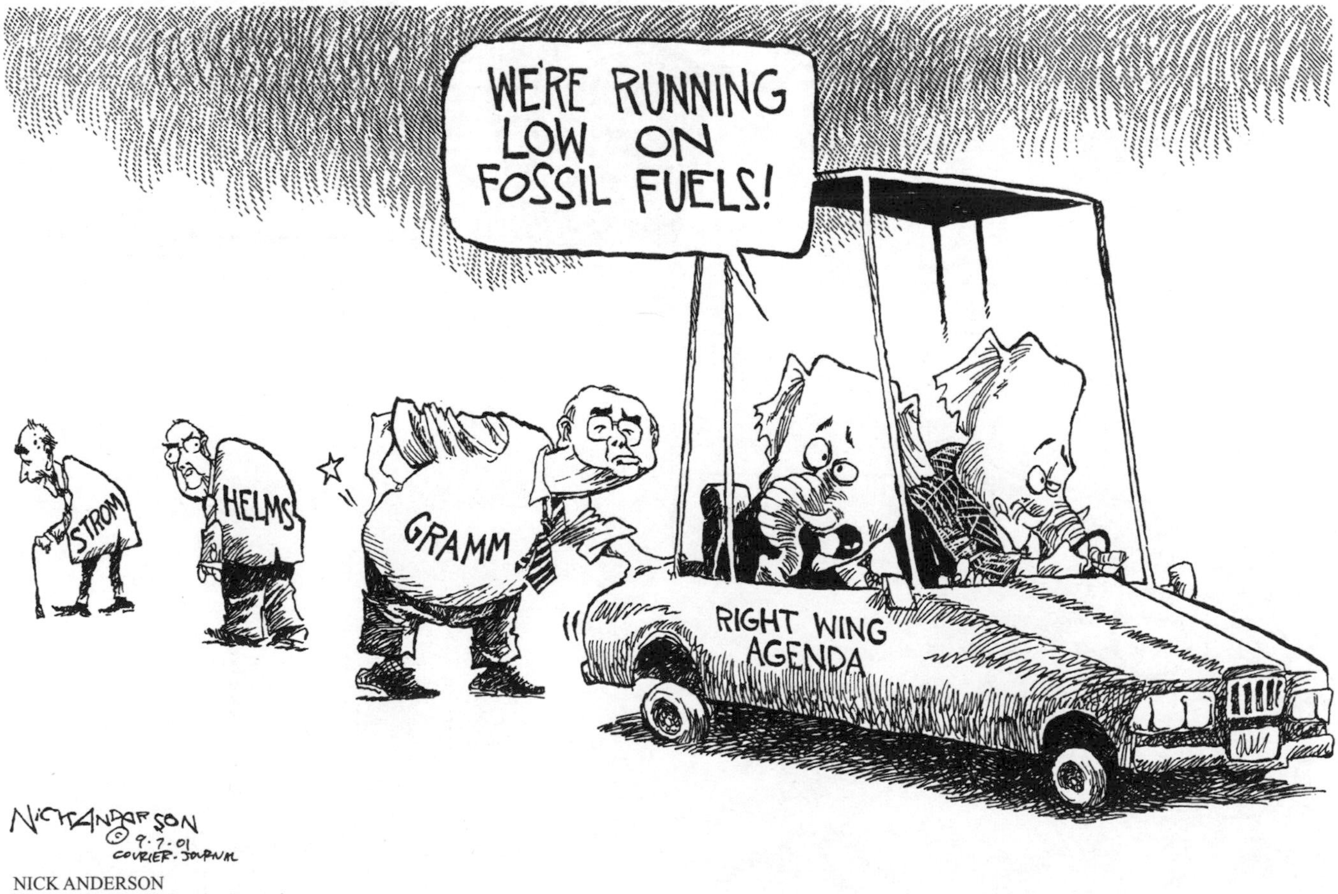
WE'RE RUNNING
LOW ON
FOSSIL FUELS!
STROM
HELMS
GRAMM
RIGHT WING
AGENDA
NICK ANDERSON © 9-7-01 COURIER-JOURNAL

NICK ANDERSON
Courtesy Louisville Courier-Journal

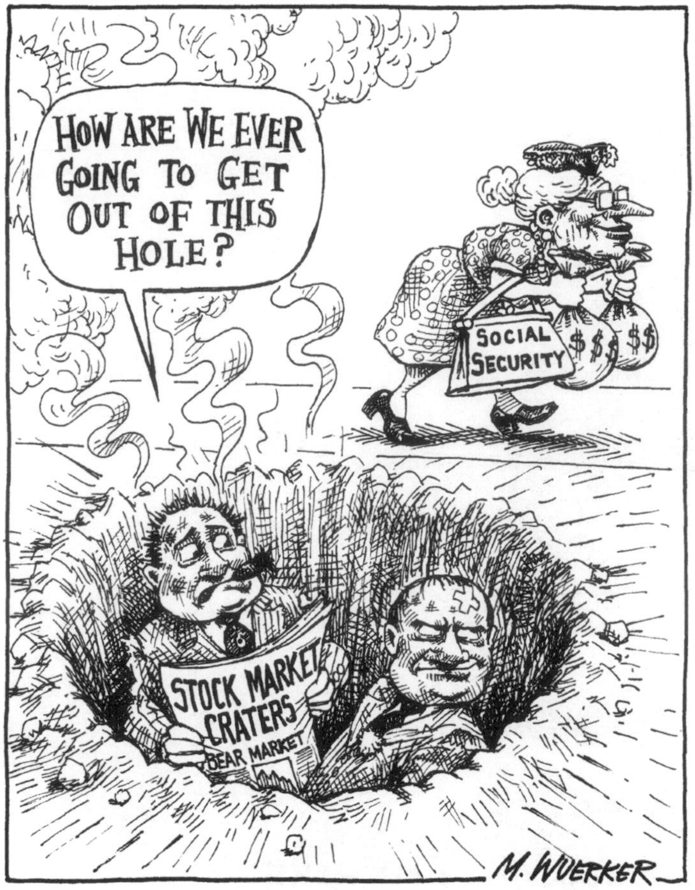
HOW ARE WE EVER GOING TO GET OUT OF THIS HOLE?
SOCIAL SECURITY
$$$
STOCK MARKET CRATERS
BEAR MARKET
M. WUERKER

MATT WUERKER
Courtesy Santa Cruz Metro

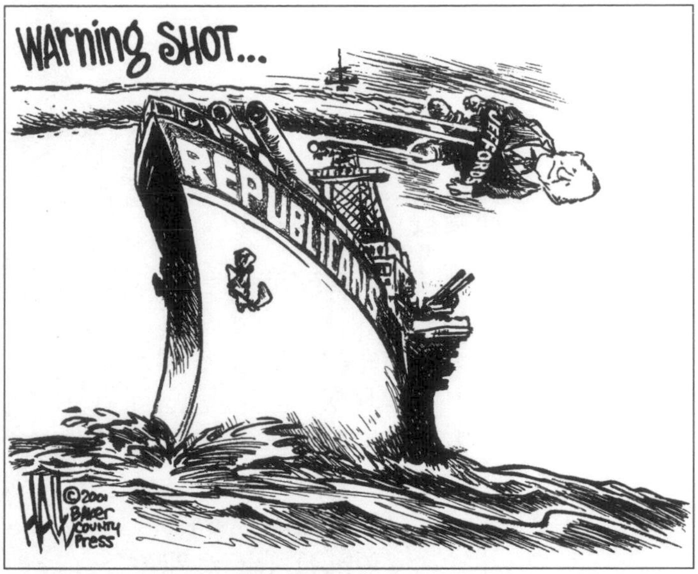
Warning SHOT...
REPUBLICANS
©2001 Baker County Press

ED HALL
Courtesy Baker County Press

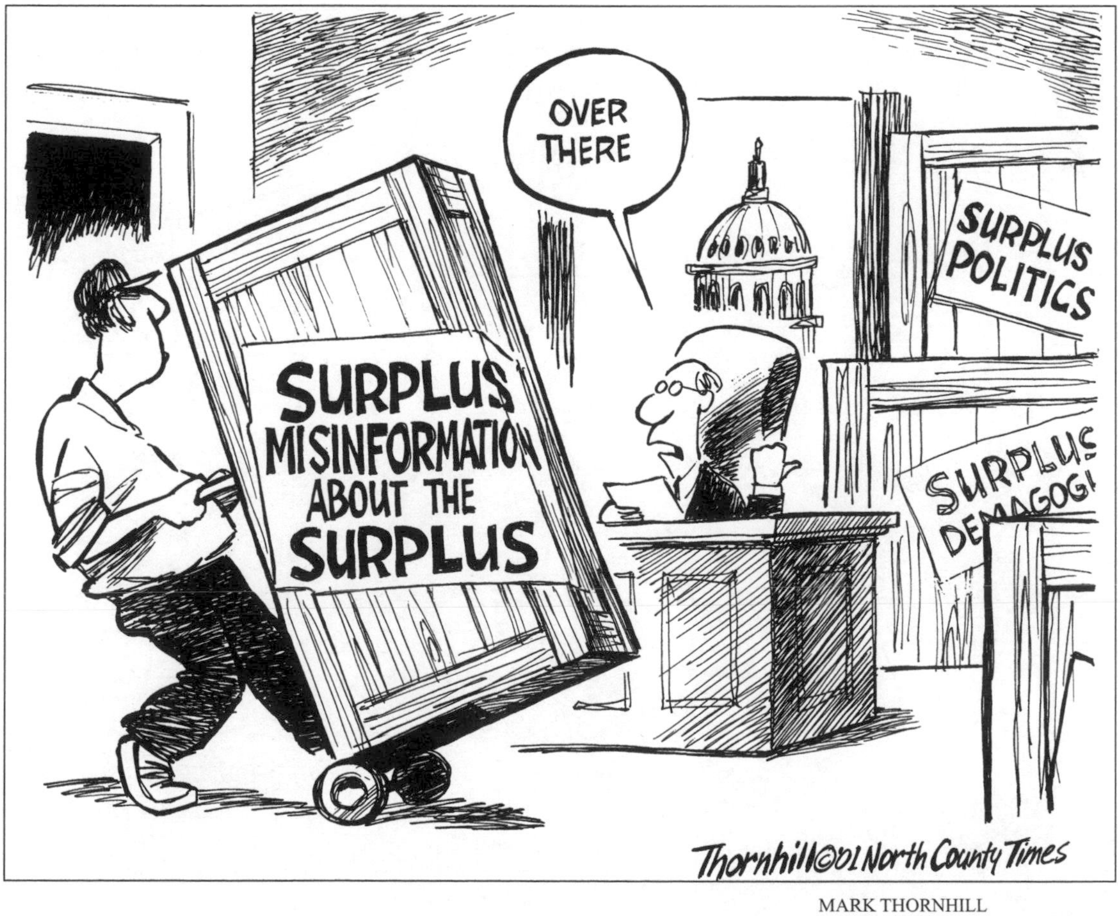
OVER THERE
SURPLUS MISINFORMATION ABOUT THE SURPLUS
SURPLUS POLITICS
Thornhill©01 North County Times

MARK THORNHILL
Courtesy North County Times (Calif.)

BILL GARNER
Courtesy Washington Times

S.C. RAWLS
Courtesy Rockdale Citizen

Crime

The execution of mass murderer Timothy McVeigh, the Oklahoma bomber, became a media circus amid speculation that his death would be broadcast on the Internet. Attorney General John Ashcroft granted permission to survivors of the bombing to watch the execution. A few days before the scheduled date, however, the FBI disclosed that it had failed to release thousands of documents to the McVeigh defense, and the execution was postponed. The sentence was finally carried out a month later.

The FBI also admitted that it had misplaced 449 guns and 184 laptop computers, at least one of which contained classified material.

FBI agent Robert Hanssen was arrested and charged with spying for Russia. He was accused of handing over classified documents to Soviet agents and revealing the names of double agents working in what was then the Soviet Union. Hanssen pleaded guilty to fifteen counts of espionage and conspiracy.

The city of Cincinnati erupted in violence after a policeman shot an unarmed black man. Black leaders accused the police of systematic racial profiling.

VIC HARVILLE
Courtesy Donrey News (Ark.)

153

LARRY WRIGHT
Courtesy Detroit News

BARBARA BRANDON-CROFT
Courtesy Universal Press Syndicate

CHARLES DANIEL
Courtesy Knoxville News-Sentinel

154

RICK McKEE
Courtesy Augusta Chronicle (Ga.)

KEVIN KALLAUGHER
Courtesy Baltimore Sun

LARRY WRIGHT
Courtesy Detroit News

DAVID DONAR
Courtesy Macomb Daily

BILL WHITEHEAD
Courtesy Kansas City Business Journal

BILL YORTH
Courtesy Waukesha Freeman (Wis.)

JOHN WEISS
Courtesy Santa Cruz Sentinel

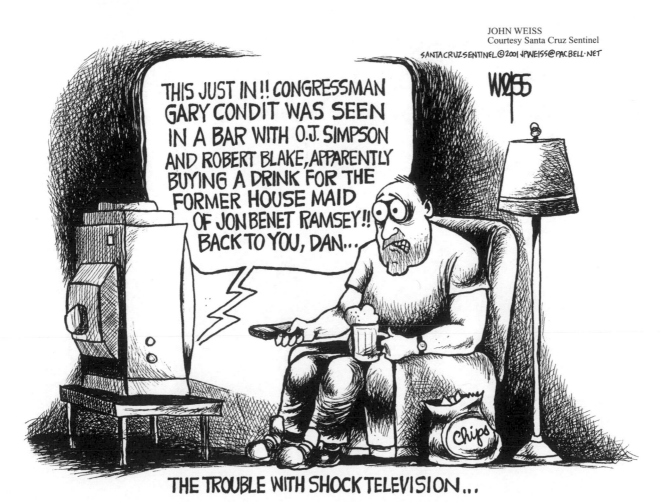

STEVE LINDSTROM
Courtesy Duluth News-Tribune

JACK HIGGINS
Courtesy Chicago Sun-Times

Society

One thing the terrorists accomplished in their September 11 attack was to bring the people of the United States together. Nationalities and colors and cultures became ONE. People clearly began to feel warmer and friendlier toward each other, and even seem to have a greater trust in government. Countless numbers of citizens looked for ways to assist in the struggle back to normalcy and donated hundreds of millions of dollars to the families of victims.

According to 2000 census figures released in 2001, the number of Americans grew by some 270 percent during the twentieth century, with non-whites increasing nearly tenfold. In fact, Hispanics surpassed blacks as a share of the total U.S. population. The number of Hispanics in the U.S. is now greater than the entire population of Canada.

In the aftermath of the terrorist attacks, many Americans expressed growing concern about the possibility of giving up some civil liberties—at airports and elsewhere—in the interest of greater security.

The U.S. is more suburban, mobile, and wired, of course, than it was in 1900, and household amenities have spread to just about everyone. Cell phone usage while driving has become a serious traffic problem, along with other gadgets that can distract drivers.

MICHAEL RAMIREZ
Courtesy Los Angeles Times

Area travel agencies try to cope with customers' security concerns.

JOHN SHERFFIUS
Courtesy St. Louis Post-Dispatch

St. Louis Post-Dispatch © 9-16-01 STLtoday.com

INDIAN-AMERICANS NORWEGIAN-AME
GERMAN-AMERICANS BOSNIAN-AMERI
AFRICAN-AMERICANS CATHOLIC AMER
ARMENIAN-AMERICANS ITALIAN-AME
SWEDISH-AMERICANS PAKISTANI-AME

ARAB-AMERICANS ANGLO-AMERICANS
KOREAN-AMERICANS IRISH-AMERICAN
POLISH-AMERICANS CHINESE-AMERIC
MEXICAN-AMERICANS CUBAN-AMERIC
VIETNAMESE-AMERICANS LEBANESE-A
JAPANESE-AMERICANS PROTESTANT AN

MERICANS JEWISH AMERICANS TURKISH-AMERICANS NATIVE AMERICANS ASIAN
TAIWANESE-AMERICANS CANADIAN-AMERICANS MUSLIM AMERICANS PERSIAN
ANS FRANCO-AMERICANS EGYPTIAN-AMERICANS DANISH-AMERICANS SWISS
M SYRIAN-AMERICANS SERBIAN-AMERICANS HAITIAN-AMERICANS SPANISH

JEFF PARKER
Courtesy Florida Today

IN LIGHT OF RECENT EVENTS, WE'RE **ALL** NEW YORKERS...

JIM BORGMAN
Courtesy Cincinnati Enquirer

BARBARA BRANDON-CROFT
Courtesy Universal Press Syndicate

BRUCE QUAST
Courtesy Rockford Register-Star

162

DANIEL FENECH
Courtesy Saline Reporter

STEVE KELLEY
Courtesy San Diego Union-Tribune

ETTA HULME
Courtesy Fort Worth Star-Telegram

PAUL FELL
Courtesy Lincoln Journal Star (Neb.)

JOE MAJESKI
Courtesy The Times Leader (Pa.)

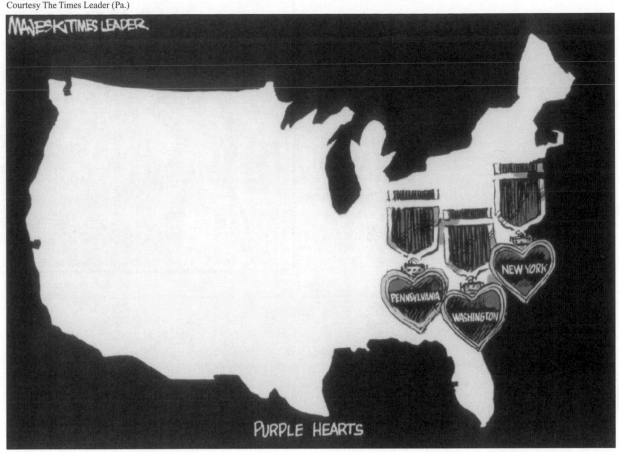

CINDY PROCIOUS
Courtesy Huntsville Times

CHIP BECK
Courtesy The Real Washington

DAVID HITCH
Courtesy Worcester Telegram and Gazette

JIM BORGMAN
Courtesy Cincinnati Enquirer

"ISN'T THERE SOME OBNOXIOUS HEAVY METAL ROCK STATION WE COULD WAKE UP TO INSTEAD OF THE NEWS FOR AWHILE?"

RICK TUMA
Courtesy Chicago Tribune

FRANK CAMMUSO
Courtesy Syracuse Herald-Journal

SCOTT NICKEL
Courtesy Antelope Valley Press

Mrs. Walton finds an effective way to communicate with her husband.

ED COLLEY
Courtesy Kingston Reporter

KIRK ANDERSON
Courtesy St. Paul Pioneer Press

CINDY PROCIOUS
Courtesy Huntsville Times

CLAY JONES
Courtesy Free Lance Star (Va.)

ANNETTE BALESTERI
Courtesy Ledger-Dispatch (Calif.)

REX BABIN
Courtesy Sacramento Bee

DANA SUMMERS
Courtesy Orlando Sentinel

JERRY HOLBERT
Courtesy Boston Herald

ETTA HULME
Courtesy Fort Worth Star-Telegram

ART HENRIKSON
Courtesy Des Plaines Daily Herald (Ill.)

JOHN DEERING
Courtesy Arkansas Democrat

UNCLE SAM'S NEW LOOK

IF YOU WANT TO TAKE AWAY MY CELL PHONE, YOU'LL HAVE TO PRY IT FROM MY COLD, DEAD FINGERS

CHARLOS GARY
Courtesy Chicago Tribune & DBR Media

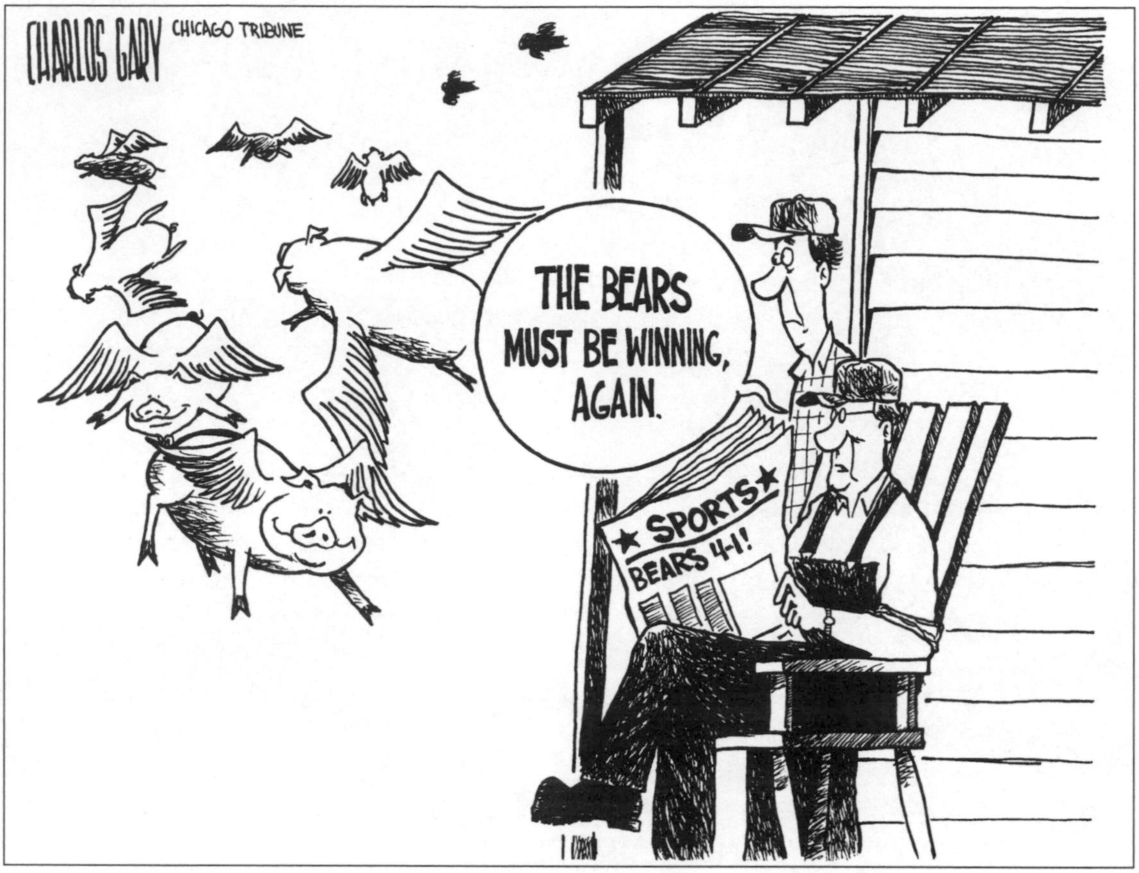
CHARLOS GARY CHICAGO TRIBUNE
THE BEARS MUST BE WINNING, AGAIN.
★ SPORTS ★
BEARS 4-1!

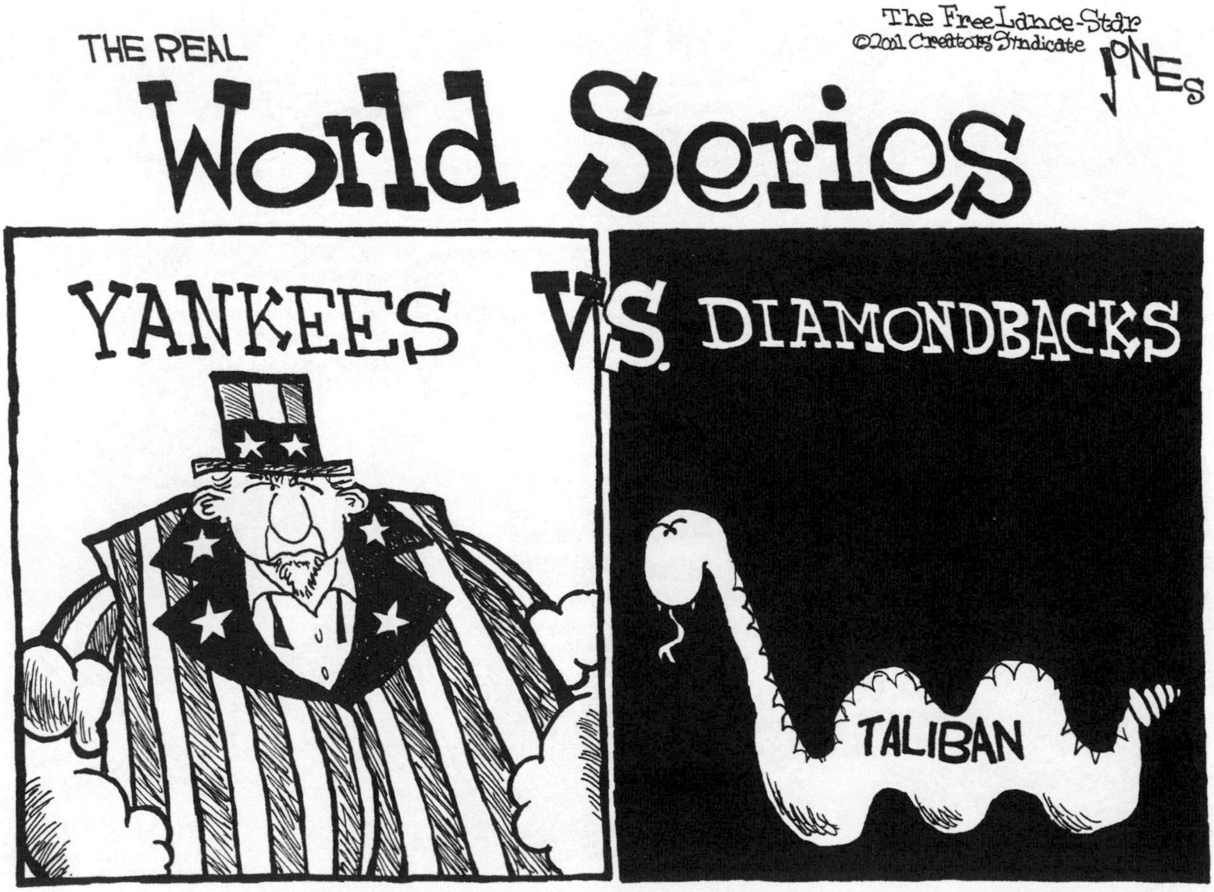
The Free Lance-Star
©2001 Creators Syndicate
JONES
THE REAL
World Series
YANKEES VS. DIAMONDBACKS
TALIBAN

CLAY JONES
Courtesy Free Lance Star (Va.)

Sports

Race driver Dale Earnhardt, who was to NASCAR fans what Michael Jordan is to National Basketball Association enthusiasts, was killed in April in a crash near the finish line of the Daytona 500. The resulting outpouring of grief across the nation rivaled that shown following the death of Elvis Presley. Memorial services were televised throughout the U.S., there were pilgrimages, and the media gave the event star coverage. Son Dale Earnhardt, Jr., won the Pepsi 400 later in the year.

The International Olympic Committee announced that the 2008 Olympic Games would be held in Beijing, China, a nation of 1.2 billion people. There was much worldwide opposition by human rights activists, who contended China did not deserve the honor because of its poor record on human rights.

The Arizona Diamondbacks beat the New York Yankees in seven games to win baseball's World Series. Slugger Mark McGwire announced his retirement because of a bum right knee that had plagued him all year. He had set a record of 70 home runs during the 1998 season. In 2001, however, Barry Bonds of the San Francisco Giants eclipsed that record, slamming 73 homers.

Michael Jordan came out of retirement in 2001 to resume his professional basketball career. He had left the game in 1999.

REX BABIN
Courtesy Sacramento Bee

GRAEME MacKAY
Courtesy Hamilton Spectator (Can.)

BRUCE QUAST
Courtesy Rockford Register-Star

CHARLOS GARY
Courtesy Chicago Tribune & DBR Media

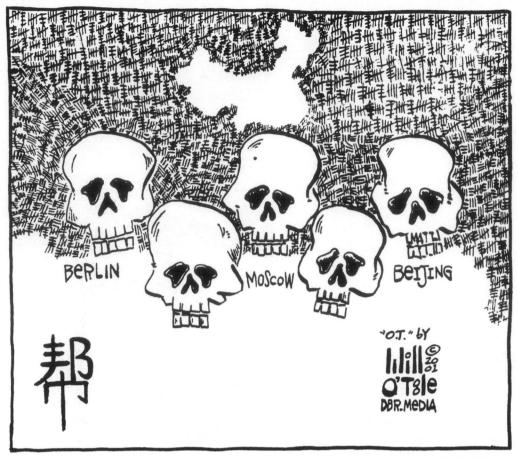

WILL O'TOOLE
Courtesy DBR Media

CHARLES DANIEL
Courtesy Knoxville News-Sentinel

JEFF STAHLER
Courtesy Cincinnati Post

BOB GORRELL
Courtesy Creators Syndicate

DAVID REDDICK
Courtesy The Herald Bulletin (Ind.)

SUGGESTED SYMBOL FOR 2008 OLYMPICS IN BEIJING

DAVID COX
Courtesy Arkansas Democrat-Gazette

WILLIAM L. FLINT
Courtesy Arlington Morning News (Tex.)

WHAT'S A LEAGUE GOTTA DO-TO GET SOME **CREDIBILITY**?

STEVE WETZEL
Courtesy Harrisburg Patriot-News

RICHARD WALLMEYER
Courtesy Long Beach Press-Telegram

ALAN VITELLO
Courtesy Greeley Tribune

Education

An unsettling trend of school violence continued through 2001. In March, a 15-year-old student at Santana High School opened fire on classmates. The incident left two dead, thirteen wounded, and another quiet suburban town torn apart. In November, another 15-year-old and two other high school students in New Bedford, Massachusetts, were charged with plotting a Columbine-style mass murder. A janitor found a note in a school corridor detailing a specific plan for bombings and shootings at the school.

In a breakthrough for President Bush's education bill late in the year, key lawmakers reached agreement on two central points—one approving annual math and reading tests for students, the other loosening the strings on billions of dollars in federal funds.

Something else—something remarkable—occurred in schools across America during the year. Following the terrorist attacks on September 11, old-fashioned patriotism and God were welcomed back into many schools where for years both had been ostracized.

WAYNE STAYSKAL
Courtesy Tampa Tribune

181

JOHN KNUDSEN
Courtesy St. Louis Review

SEPARATION OF COMMON SENSE AND STATE

CHAN LOWE
Courtesy Fort Lauderdale News/Sun Sentinel

DAVE SATTLER
Courtesy Lafayette Journal and Courier

ED GAMBLE
Courtesy Florida Times-Union

ANN CLEAVES
Courtesy Palisadian Post

STEVE WETZEL
Courtesy Harrisburg Patriot-News

ALAN VITELLO
Courtesy Greeley Tribune

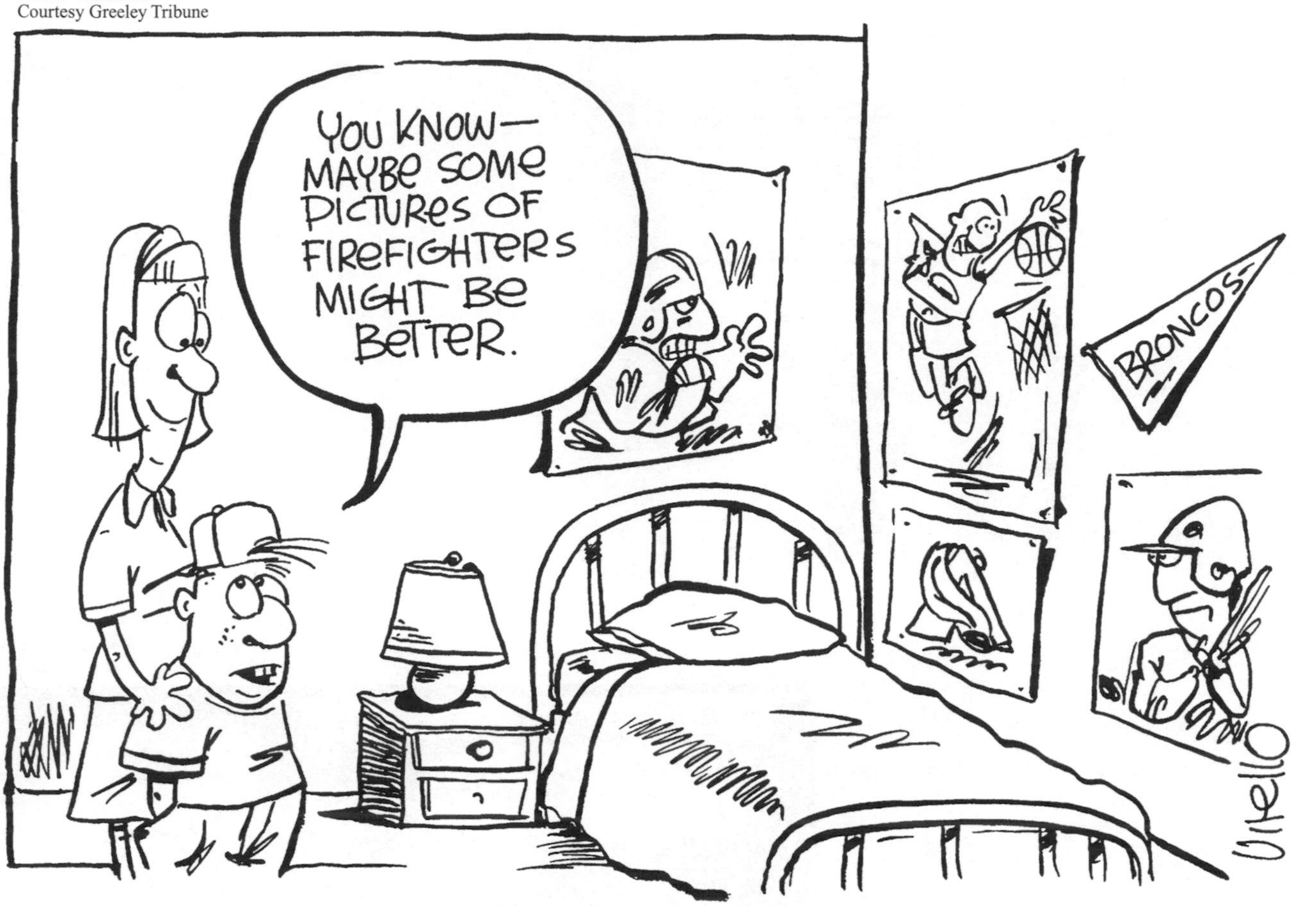
YOU KNOW—
MAYBE SOME
PICTURES OF
FIREFIGHTERS
MIGHT BE
BETTER.
BRONCOS
VITELLO

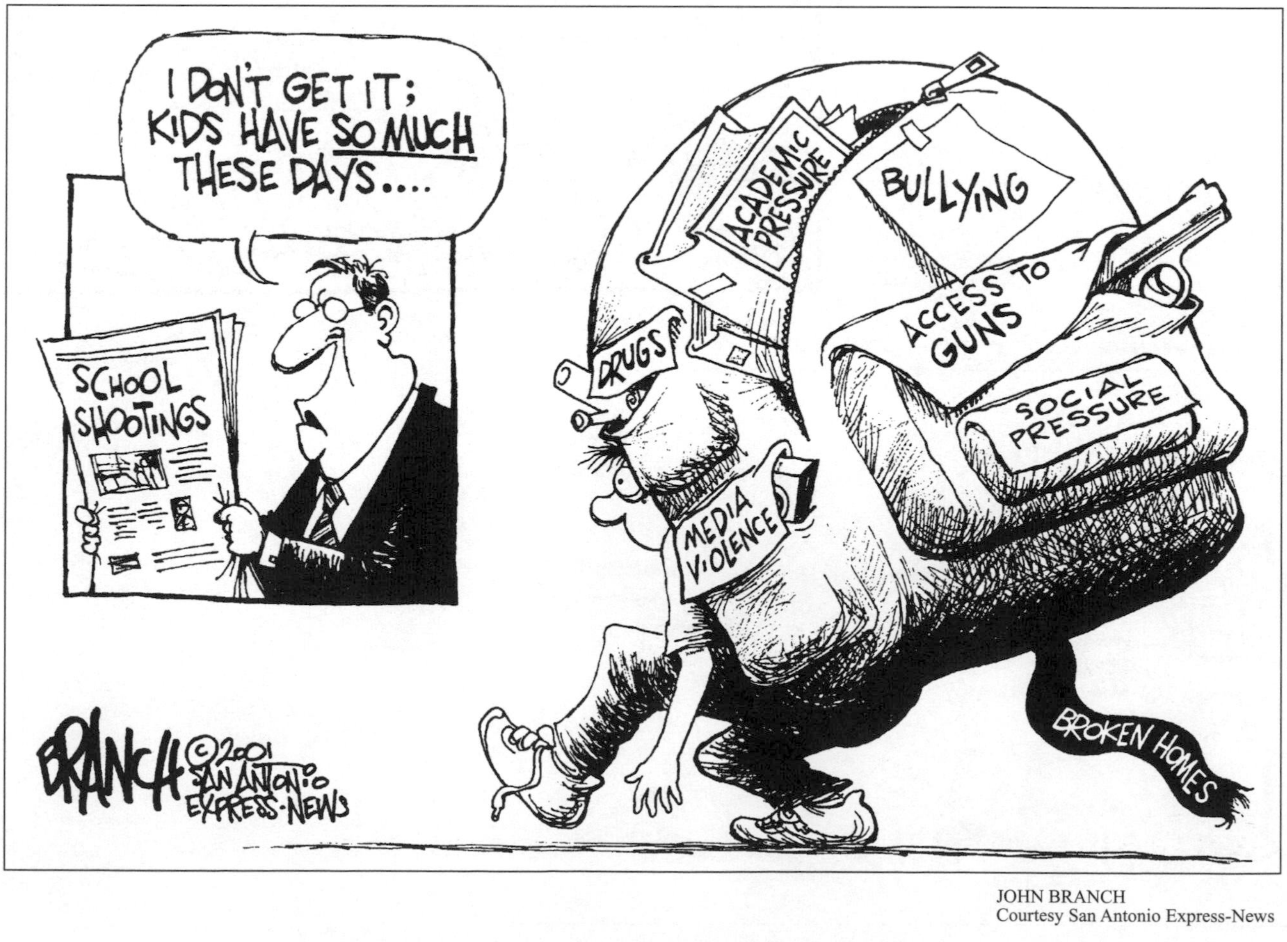
I DON'T GET IT;
KIDS HAVE SO MUCH
THESE DAYS....
SCHOOL SHOOTINGS
ACADEMIC PRESSURE
BULLYING
ACCESS TO GUNS
DRUGS
SOCIAL PRESSURE
MEDIA VIOLENCE
BROKEN HOMES
BRANCH ©2001 SAN ANTONIO EXPRESS-NEWS

JOHN BRANCH
Courtesy San Antonio Express-News

Space and Air Travel

The airline industry appeared to have been the hardest hit by the terrorist attacks on New York City. People naturally were apprehensive about flying, and even with huge sums of assistance from the government, airlines faced a difficult future. Traditional airline passengers were beginning to return, but nationwide airline travel remained down about 25 percent.

Uniformed National Guardsmen are providing airport security, and checkpoints are being more closely watched. All airlines have assured the public they have strengthened cockpit doors and enhanced other forms of security. Passengers can now expect to take some two hours to get through checkpoints for domestic flights and some three hours for international flights.

The decrepit space station MIR was crash-landed by Russia in the southern Pacific Ocean after fifteen years in orbit around the earth. About 1,500 chunks weighing forty pounds or more rained down on the ocean during reentry. MIR, which had made 86,331 orbits around the globe, had become too costly and too dangerous and was no longer needed.

ED GAMBLE
Courtesy Florida Times-Union

(MIR station falls into the Pacific Ocean as the last episode of "Survivor" airs on television.)

What are the odds...?

SURVIVOR

GUY BADEAUX
Courtesy Le Droit (Can.)

JONATHAN TODD
Courtesy Metrowest Daily News (Mass.)

U.S. AIRPORT SECURITY

TERRORISTS

TODD 2001
METROWEST
DAILY NEWS

DOORS

HOMES

APT.

BANKS

COCKPITS

TIMER

ALARM

ANNETTE BALESTERI
Courtesy Ledger-Dispatch (Calif.)

JOE MAJESKI
Courtesy The Times Leader (Pa.)

FALLING OUT OF ORBIT

BILL WHITEHEAD
Courtesy Kansas City Business Journal

ERIC SMITH
Courtesy Annapolis Capital-Gazette

W.A. HOGAN
Courtesy St. John Telegraph Journal (Can.)

JACK CHAPMAN
Courtesy Desoto Times Today

Canada

Protesters at the Summit of the Americas, registering their opposition to free trade and globalization, threw bricks, pipes, and hockey pucks at police officers, who responded with smoke and tear gas canisters. The confrontation between an estimated 1,000 protesters and 150 police officers delayed the start of a three-day meeting of leaders from throughout the hemisphere.

A revolt within Canada's main opposition group spread to the party's top leadership, with some members of the Canadian Alliance's national executive committee asking for the resignation of leader Stockwell Day. Day was accused of being an unqualified and autocratic leader.

Prime Minister Jean Chrétien assured President Bush that Canada was ready to assist in any way in the fight against terrorism.

The Canadian Fisheries minister hauled a group of Indians into court in a dispute over lobster fishing, and the government ended up paying the defendants' legal fees. In New Brunswick, descendants of the Acadians demanded that Queen Elizabeth apologize for their expulsion 200 years ago. There was also a big dispute between lumber lobby groups in Canada and the U.S. over the issue of free trade.

W.A. HOGAN
Courtesy St. John Telegraph Journal (Can.)

ROY PETERSON
Courtesy Vancouver Sun

STEVE NEASE
Courtesy London Free Press (Can.)

ROY PETERSON
Courtesy Vancouver Sun

STEVE NEASE
Courtesy Niagara Falls Review

THE WATERBOY

TIM DOLIGHAN
Courtesy Toronto Sun

STEVE NEASE
Courtesy Toronto Sun

W.A. HOGAN
Courtesy St. John Telegraph Journal (Can.)

GRAEME MacKAY
Courtesy Hamilton Spectator (Can.)

... and Other Issues

Two hugely controversial issues made headlines during the year: human cloning and stem cell research. Despite a House-passed ban on human cloning, scientists insisted they were determined to go ahead with their efforts. President Bush approved limited funding for stem cell research, a process that is controversial because it involves the destruction of human embryos.

A team of scientists was able to grow human muscle and bone from adult stem cells. In late December, a Boston research company reported that it had cloned the first human embryo.

California ordered utilities companies to cut off electricity to hundreds of thousands of customers in the first rolling blackouts imposed during the state's months-long energy crisis. California has not built a power plant in more than ten years and has been buying electricity from other states.

The trouble-plagued FBI suffered another black eye when it was revealed that the agency had misplaced a large inventory of weapons and supplies.

Many noted figures passed away during the year, including Dr. Christian Barnard, Jack Lemmon, Anthony Quinn, Perry Como, Dale Earnhardt, Dale Evans, and cartoonists Fred Laswell, Herbert Block, Hank Ketcham, Tom Darcy, Edgar Soller, and Charles Bissell.

DICK LOCHER
Courtesy Chicago Tribune

ETTA HULME
Courtesy Fort Worth Star-Telegram

J.R. ROSE
Courtesy Byrd Newspapers

JEFF STAHLER
Courtesy Cincinnati Post

CHUCK ASAY
Courtesy Colorado Springs Gazette-Telegraph

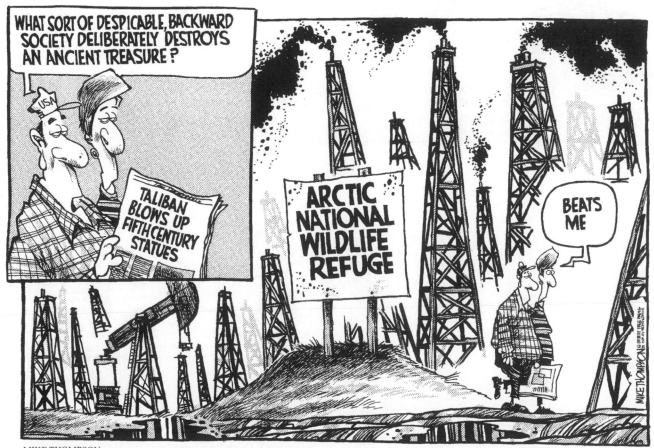

MIKE THOMPSON
Courtesy Detroit Free Press

STACY CURTIS
Courtesy MSNBC & The Times

STEPHEN TEMPLETON
Courtesy Fayetteville Observer-Times

MICHAEL CAVNA
Courtesy San Diego Union-Tribune

196

STEVE McBRIDE
Courtesy Independence Daily Reporter (Kan.)

JAMES CASCIARI
Courtesy Vero Beach Press Journal

TOM BECK
Courtesy Freeport Journal-Standard (Ill.)

BILL VALLADARES
Courtesy Montclair Times (N.J.)

BOB LANG
Courtesy The News-Sentinel (Ind.)

VIC HARVILLE
Courtesy Donrey News (Ark.)

MIKE LUCKOVICH
Courtesy Atlanta Constitution

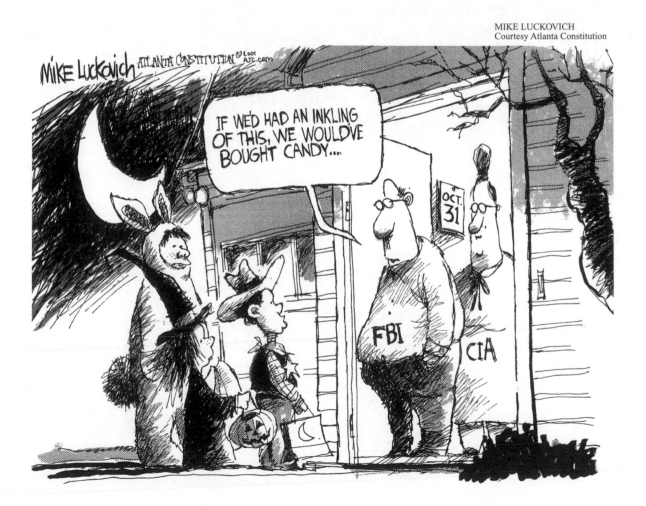

DANIEL FENECH
Courtesy Saline Reporter

JERRY BARNETT
Courtesy Indianapolis Star

RICHARD CROWSON
Courtesy Wichita Eagle

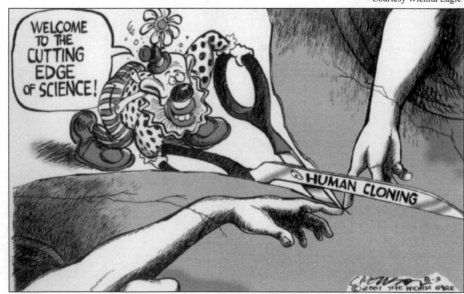

CHAN LOWE
Courtesy Fort Lauderdale News/Sun Sentinel

GARY MARKSTEIN
Courtesy Milwaukee Journal Sentinel

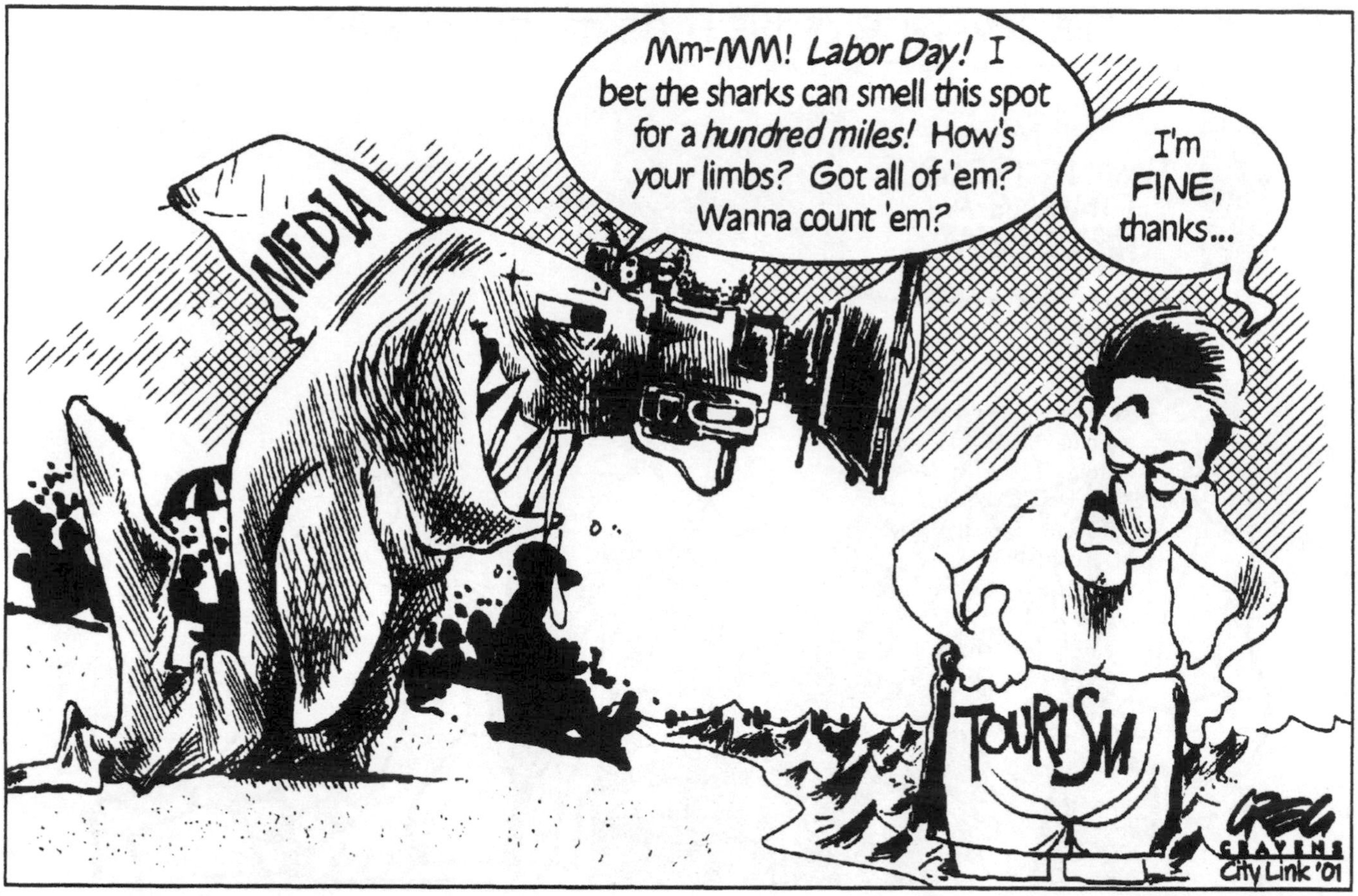
Mm-MM! Labor Day! I bet the sharks can smell this spot for a hundred miles! How's your limbs? Got all of 'em? Wanna count 'em?
I'm FINE, thanks...
MEDIA
TOURISM
GREG CRAVENS
City Link '01

GREG CRAVENS
Courtesy ANG Newspapers

DOUG REGALIA
Courtesy Contra Costa Sun

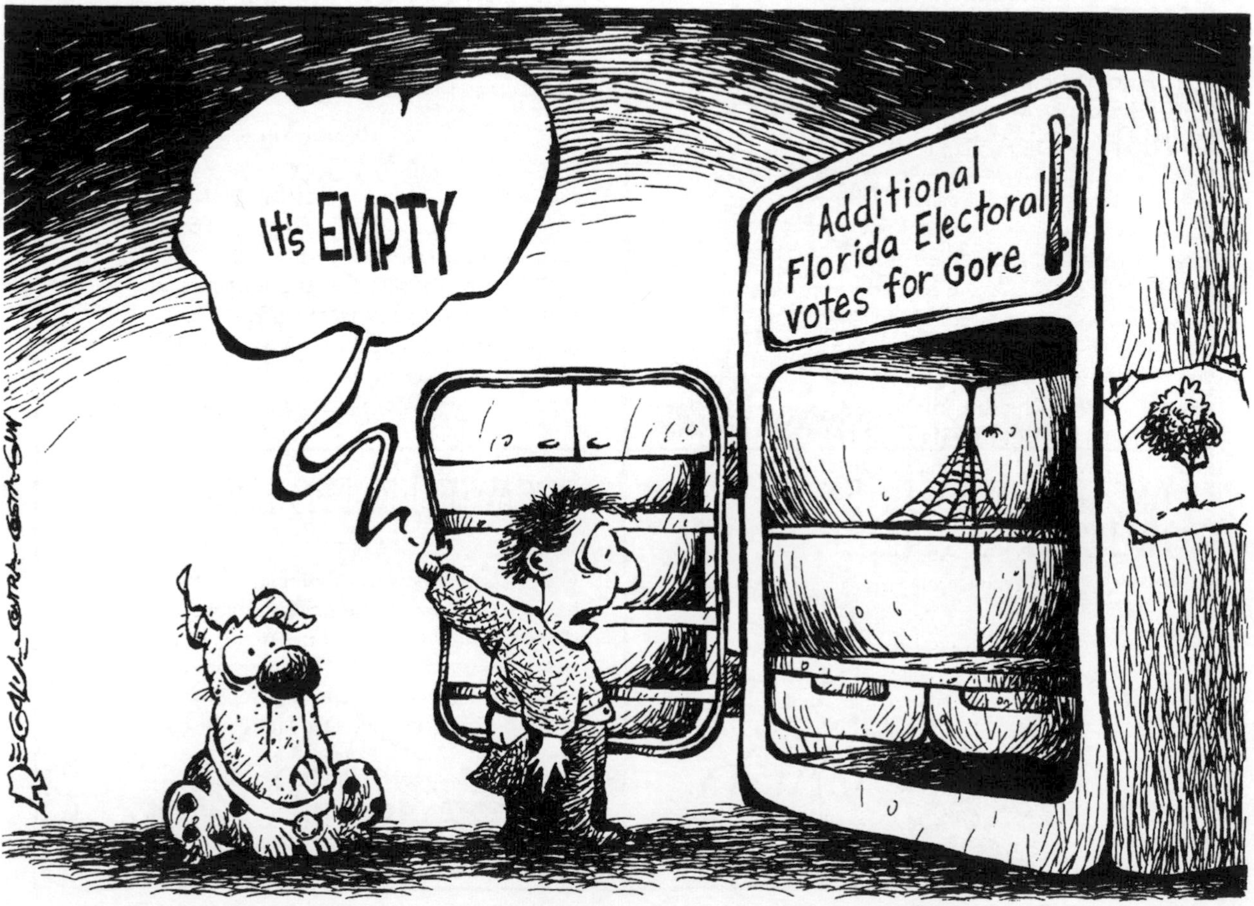
It's EMPTY
Additional Florida Electoral votes for Gore

Past Award Winners

PULITZER PRIZE

1922—Rollin Kirby, New York World
1923—No award given
1924—J.N. Darling, New York Herald-Tribune
1925—Rollin Kirby, New York World
1926—D.R. Fitzpatrick, St. Louis Post-Dispatch
1927—Nelson Harding, Brooklyn Eagle
1928—Nelson Harding, Brooklyn Eagle
1929—Rollin Kirby, New York World
1930—Charles Macauley, Brooklyn Eagle
1931—Edmund Duffy, Baltimore Sun
1932—John T. McCutcheon, Chicago Tribune
1933—H.M. Talburt, Washington Daily News
1934—Edmund Duffy, Baltimore Sun
1935—Ross A. Lewis, Milwaukee Journal
1936—No award given
1937—C.D. Batchelor, New York Daily News
1938—Vaughn Shoemaker, Chicago Daily News
1939—Charles G. Werner, Daily Oklahoman
1940—Edmund Duffy, Baltimore Sun
1941—Jacob Burck, Chicago Times
1942—Herbert L. Block, NEA
1943—Jay N. Darling, New York Herald-Tribune
1944—Clifford K. Berryman, Washington Star
1945—Bill Mauldin, United Features Syndicate
1946—Bruce Russell, Los Angeles Times
1947—Vaughn Shoemaker, Chicago Daily News
1948—Reuben L. ("Rube") Goldberg, New York Sun
1949—Lute Pease, Newark Evening News
1950—James T. Berryman, Washington Star
1951—Reginald W. Manning, Arizona Republic
1952—Fred L. Packer, New York Mirror
1953—Edward D. Kuekes, Cleveland Plain Dealer
1954—Herbert L. Block, Washington Post
1955—Daniel R. Fitzpatrick, St. Louis Post-Dispatch
1956—Robert York, Louisville Times
1957—Tom Little, Nashville Tennessean
1958—Bruce M. Shanks, Buffalo Evening News
1959—Bill Mauldin, St. Louis Post-Dispatch
1960—No award given
1961—Carey Orr, Chicago Tribune
1962—Edmund S. Valtman, Hartford Times
1963—Frank Miller, Des Moines Register
1964—Paul Conrad, Denver Post
1965—No award given
1966—Don Wright, Miami News
1967—Patrick B. Oliphant, Denver Post
1968—Eugene Gray Payne, Charlotte Observer
1969—John Fischetti, Chicago Daily News
1970—Thomas F. Darcy, Newsday
1971—Paul Conrad, Los Angeles Times
1972—Jeffrey K. MacNelly, Richmond News Leader
1973—No award given
1974—Paul Szep, Boston Globe
1975—Garry Trudeau, Universal Press Syndicate
1976—Tony Auth, Philadelphia Enquirer
1977—Paul Szep, Boston Globe

1978—Jeff MacNelly, Richmond News Leader
1979—Herbert Block, Washington Post
1980—Don Wright, Miami News
1981—Mike Peters, Dayton Daily News
1982—Ben Sargent, Austin American-Statesman
1983—Dick Locher, Chicago Tribune
1984—Paul Conrad, Los Angeles Times
1985—Jeff MacNelly, Chicago Tribune
1986—Jules Feiffer, Universal Press Syndicate
1987—Berke Breathed, Washington Post Writers Group
1988—Doug Marlette, Atlanta Constitution
1989—Jack Higgins, Chicago Sun-Times
1990—Tom Toles, Buffalo News
1991—Jim Borgman, Cincinnati Enquirer
1992—Signe Wilkinson, Philadelphia Daily News
1993—Steve Benson, Arizona Republic
1994—Michael Ramirez, Memphis Commercial Appeal
1995—Mike Luckovich, Atlanta Constitution
1996—Jim Morin, Miami Herald
1997—Walt Handelsman, New Orleans Times-Picayune
1998—Steve Breen, Asbury Park Press
1999—David Horsey, Seattle Post-Intelligencer
2000—Joel Pett, Lexington Herald-Leader
2001—Ann Telnaes, Tribune Media Services

NATIONAL SOCIETY OF PROFESSIONAL JOURNALISTS AWARD (SIGMA DELTA CHI AWARD)

1942—Jacob Burck, Chicago Times
1943—Charles Werner, Chicago Sun
1944—Henry Barrow, Associated Press
1945—Reuben L. Goldberg, New York Sun
1946—Dorman H. Smith, NEA
1947—Bruce Russell, Los Angeles Times
1948—Herbert Block, Washington Post
1949—Herbert Block, Washington Post
1950—Bruce Russell, Los Angeles Times
1951—Herbert Block, Washington Post and
        Bruce Russell, Los Angeles Times
1952—Cecil Jensen, Chicago Daily News
1953—John Fischetti, NEA
1954—Calvin Alley, Memphis Commercial Appeal
1955—John Fischetti, NEA
1956—Herbert Block, Washington Post
1957—Scott Long, Minneapolis Tribune
1958—Clifford H. Baldowski, Atlanta Constitution
1959—Charles G. Brooks, Birmingham News
1960—Dan Dowling, New York Herald-Tribune
1961—Frank Interlandi, Des Moines Register
1962—Paul Conrad, Denver Post
1963—William Mauldin, Chicago Sun-Times
1964—Charles Bissell, Nashville Tennessean
1965—Roy Justus, Minneapolis Star
1966—Patrick Oliphant, Denver Post

1967—Eugene Payne, Charlotte Observer
1968—Paul Conrad, Los Angeles Times
1969—William Mauldin, Chicago Sun-Times
1970—Paul Conrad, Los Angeles Times
1971—Hugh Haynie, Louisville Courier-Journal
1972—William Mauldin, Chicago Sun-Times
1973—Paul Szep, Boston Globe
1974—Mike Peters, Dayton Daily News
1975—Tony Auth, Philadelphia Enquirer
1976—Paul Szep, Boston Globe
1977—Don Wright, Miami News
1978—Jim Borgman, Cincinnati Enquirer
1979—John P. Trever, Albuquerque Journal
1980—Paul Conrad, Los Angeles Times
1981—Paul Conrad, Los Angeles Times
1982—Dick Locher, Chicago Tribune
1983—Rob Lawlor, Philadelphia Daily News
1984—Mike Lane, Baltimore Evening Sun
1985—Doug Marlette, Charlotte Observer
1986—Mike Keefe, Denver Post
1987—Paul Conrad, Los Angeles Times
1988—Jack Higgins, Chicago Sun-Times
1989—Don Wright, Palm Beach Post
1990—Jeff MacNelly, Chicago Tribune
1991—Walt Handelsman, New Orleans Times-Picayune
1992—Robert Ariail, Columbia State
1993—Herbert Block, Washington Post
1994—Jim Borgman, Cincinnati Enquirer
1995—Michael Ramirez, Memphis Commercial Appeal
1996—Paul Conrad, Los Angeles Times
1997—Michael Ramirez, Los Angeles Times
1998—Jack Higgins, Chicago Sun-Times
1999—Mike Thompson, Detroit Free Press
2000—Nick Anderson, Louisville Courier-Journal

NATIONAL NEWSPAPER AWARD/CANADA

1949—Jack Boothe, Toronto Globe and Mail
1950—James G. Reidford, Montreal Star
1951—Len Norris, Vancouver Sun
1952—Robert La Palme, Le Devoir, Montreal
1953—Robert W. Chambers, Halifax Chronicle-Herald
1954—John Collins, Montreal Gazette
1955—Merle R. Tingley, London Free Press

1956—James G. Reidford, Toronto Globe and Mail
1957—James G. Reidford, Toronto Globe and Mail
1958—Raoul Hunter, Le Soleil, Quebec
1959—Duncan Macpherson, Toronto Star
1960—Duncan Macpherson, Toronto Star
1961—Ed McNally, Montreal Star
1962—Duncan Macpherson, Toronto Star
1963—Jan Kamienski, Winnipeg Tribune
1964—Ed McNally, Montreal Star
1965—Duncan Macpherson, Toronto Star
1966—Robert W. Chambers, Halifax Chronicle-Herald
1967—Raoul Hunter, Le Soleil, Quebec
1968—Roy Peterson, Vancouver Sun
1969—Edward Uluschak, Edmonton Journal
1970—Duncan Macpherson, Toronto Daily Star
1971—Yardley Jones, Toronto Daily Star
1972—Duncan Macpherson, Toronto Star
1973—John Collins, Montreal Gazette
1974—Blaine, Hamilton Spectator
1975—Roy Peterson, Vancouver Sun
1976—Andy Donato, Toronto Sun
1977—Terry Mosher, Montreal Gazette
1978—Terry Mosher, Montreal Gazette
1979—Edd Uluschak, Edmonton Journal
1980—Vic Roschkov, Toronto Star
1981—Tom Innes, Calgary Herald
1982—Blaine, Hamilton Spectator
1983—Dale Cummings, Winnipeg Free Press
1984—Roy Peterson, Vancouver Sun
1985—Ed Franklin, Toronto Globe and Mail
1986—Brian Gable, Regina Leader-Post
1987—Raffi Anderian, Ottawa Citizen
1988—Vance Rodewalt, Calgary Herald
1989—Cameron Cardow, Regina Leader-Post
1990—Roy Peterson, Vancouver Sun
1991—Guy Badeaux, Le Droit, Ottawa
1992—Bruce Mackinnon, Halifax Herald
1993—Bruce Mackinnon, Halifax Herald
1994—Roy Peterson, Vancouver Sun
1995—Brian Gable, Toronto Globe and Mail
1996—Roy Peterson, Vancouver Sun
1997—Serge Chapleau, La Presse
1998—Roy Peterson, Vancouver Sun
1999—Serge Chapleau, La Presse
2000—Serge Chapleau, La Presse

Index of Cartoonists

INDEX OF CARTOONISTS

Complete Your CARTOON COLLECTION

Previous editions of this timeless classic are available for those wishing to update their collection of the most provocative moments of the past three decades. In the early days the topics were the oil crisis, Richard Nixon's presidency, Watergate, and the Vietnam War. Those subjects have given way to the Clinton impeachment trial, the historic 2000 presidential election, and the terrorist attack on America. Most important, in the end, the wit and wisdom of the editorial cartoonists prevail on the pages of these op-ed editorials, where one can find memories and much, much more in the work of the nation's finest cartoonists.

Select from the following supply of past editions

_____ 1972 Edition $18.95 pb (F)	_____ 1984 Edition $18.95 pb (F)	_____ 1995 Edition $14.95 pb
_____ 1974 Edition $18.95 pb (F)	_____ 1985 Edition $18.95 pb (F)	_____ 1996 Edition $14.95 pb
_____ 1975 Edition $18.95 pb (F)	_____ 1986 Edition $18.95 pb (F)	_____ 1997 Edition $14.95 pb
_____ 1976 Edition $18.95 pb (F)	_____ 1987 Edition $14.95 pb	_____ 1998 Edition $14.95 pb
_____ 1977 Edition $18.95 pb (F)	_____ 1988 Edition $14.95 pb	_____ 1999 Edition $14.95 pb
_____ 1978 Edition $18.95 pb (F)	_____ 1989 Edition $18.95 pb (F)	_____ 2000 Edition $14.95 pb
_____ 1979 Edition $18.95 pb (F)	_____ 1990 Edition $14.95 pb	_____ 2001 Edition $14.95 pb
_____ 1980 Edition $18.95 pb (F)	_____ 1991 Edition $14.95 pb	_____ 2002 Edition $14.95 pb
_____ 1981 Edition $18.95 pb (F)	_____ 1992 Edition $14.95 pb	Add me to the list of stand-
_____ 1982 Edition $18.95 pb (F)	_____ 1993 Edition $14.95 pb	ing orders
_____ 1983 Edition $18.95 pb (F)	_____ 1994 Edition $14.95 pb	

Please include $2.75 for 4th Class Postage and handling or $5.35 for UPS Ground Shipment plus $.75 for each additional copy ordered.

Total enclosed: _____

NAME _____

ADDRESS _____

CITY_____STATE_____ZIP_____

Make checks payable to:

PELICAN PUBLISHING COMPANY
P.O. Box 3110, Dept. 6BEC
Gretna, Louisiana 70054-3110

CREDIT CARD ORDERS CALL 1-800-843-1724 or 1-888-5-PELICAN or go to e-pelican.com
Jefferson Parish residents add 8¾% tax. All other Louisiana residents add 4% tax.
Please visit our Web site at www.pelicanpub.com or e-mail us at sales@pelicanpub.com